Denim
and
Diamonds

◆◆◆◆◆◆◆◆

Denim
and
Diamonds

◆◆◆◆◆◆◆

THE STORY OF

Emma Lee Turney's
Round Top Antiques Fair

CO-AUTHORED BY BEVERLY HARRIS

Dedicated to My Two Mothers

Ann Lorraine Faulkner Preslar Rutherford,
Who gave me a love of all things beautiful in life,
And my foster mother, Flora Rebecca Turney,
Who believed there is only one way to do anything,
And that is the right way.
And to Lois, Thelma, Ralph, Hollis and James,
Who showed me how to enjoy life
And instilled in me an ongoing work ethic.

– Emma Lee Preslar Turney

This book is published on the occasion of
the 30th Anniversary Spring Round Top Antiques Fair.

Library of Congress Catalog Card Number 98-70304

ISBN 0-9662-005-0-0

Published by
C. Going Press
Newport, Rhode Island

Distributed by
Antiques Productions
P.O. Box 821289
Houston, Texas 77282-1289

Design
Matthew Monk, Providence, Rhode Island

Production Coordination
Susan McNally, Cambridge, Massachusetts

Printing and Binding
Tien Wah Press, Singapore

On the flap
A lady and some nice old things
Original photograph by Ted Powers
Painting from photograph by Marvin (Jeff) Jeffries
Photograph of painting by Hickey/Robertson

Contents

Garden Accessories. Photo, Hickey/Robertson

A Few Words from
Madeleine McDermott Hamm

Spending the day in the countryside, wearing jeans and sneakers, eating barbecue, basking in the bluebonnets in April and the autumn air in October, immersing yourself in endlessly curious and enticing antiques – how could this not be a bit of heaven?

Year after year, one of the best things about my job as Home Design Editor of the Houston Chronicle continues to be covering the Round Top Antiques Fairs. Certainly, I am privileged to visit and write about beautifully decorated homes and preview thousands of new sofas, chairs and tables twice a year at the gigantic International Home Furnishings Market in High Point, N.C., but Round Top remains one of my favorite assignments.

One of its best aspects is the total lack of pretense. You cannot tell who arrived in the Mercedes and who came in the faithful pickup truck, and no one cares. Everyone is a country cousin for the day. Of course, it helps to be a rich cousin. It is not a flea market. Folks come to Round Top expecting the best and ready to pay for it.

The first time I arrived at the antique Rifle Association Building back in the 1970s, I was more than a little puzzled by it all. I had been to museums, antiques shops and auctions in the city, but this country thing was completely new to me.

Since my Round Top initiation, I have gained a warm appreciation for the well-loved, often worn and increasingly valuable objects surfacing on the competitive collecting market.

Although the general term for the antiques at the Round Top show is "country," the offerings go far beyond egg crates, crocks and quilts. You can find the same porcelains and brass candlesticks sold in the city, and they are just as likely to be taken home to a high-rise condo as a weekend country cottage.

Country, I've learned, is as much an attitude as it is a style. Country is an easygoing, comfortable way of living that adapts to city life, too. It's a mixture of what pleases you.

Much of my ongoing education along these lines has been guided by the Energizer Bunny of antiques, show producer Emma Lee Turney and a number of the longtime Round Top show dealers, including Laura Ann Rau, June Worrell, Sallie and Wesley Anderson, Nancy Krause, Agatha Machamehl, Ann Gunnells and Barbara Tungate. Their obvious joy in each new treasure that passes through their hands is truly contagious.

In fact, perhaps I caught this collecting bug from them.

I was convinced I had seldom reached for my checkbook during the Round Top trips until I stopped and looked around me – at a Blue Willow platter and several Blue Willow plates, a Native American splint drying basket, a large Kilim rug, an Imari bowl, a Currier & Ives print of "Bummer," a miniature rocking chair, a small beaded basket, a framed print in the style of Maxfield Parrish, an English ironstone plate with a polychrome Oriental design and…

Well, if you're going to write about collecting, it helps to understand the subject.

– Madeleine McDermott Hamm

Charlie Ham, Montalba, Texas, is a real Texas cowboy, horseman,
art and antiques dealer. He also designed those boots he is wearing.
Photo, Hickey Robertson

Mink, Martinis and Manure

♦♦♦♦♦♦♦

That phrase was used by a Houston newspaper society and gossip columnist to describe the weekend exodus of hoards of Houstonians to the Round Top area during the 1970s.

All things change, yet remain much the same. We've come a long way since the hand-addressed show invitation days with twenty-two dealers impatient to set up in an early dance hall. Now it is first class, presorted, professionally packaged mail, with approximately three hundred dealers impatient to set up in two dance halls and two football field-sized custom tents. And since wearing fur is not quite as popular and a lot of people are more health conscious and no longer drinking and since manure has gone the way of potting soil, we decided to name the book "Denim and Diamonds" to be more in keeping with the times.

But back in the beginnings…

Houston steel industrialist Richard Schill was a colorful leader of the pack. The Schill Ranch was the scene of endless parties and his generous hospitality included an after the Round Top Fourth of July parade party for hundreds. The Schills, Richard and brother John, flew in customers from as far away as Italy and France. Later, during the summer, the Schills hosted an annual poolside party for the wives of the Texas Legislators and those of us who were members of Friends of Winedale acted as hostesses.

It was this huge contingent of fun loving Houstonians who continued their social soirees in the country. They raised prized Santa Gertrudis and Longhorn cattle to show off, not show. And they gave the writers plenty of opportunity to describe the social activities at their second homes.

It was this same group and the purist antiques collectors who joined them that lined up at the Rifle Hall for each Antiques Fair, jockeying to be first in line and first at the treasures inside. They helped create the mystique that brought the show to statewide, then national, and now, international, attention.

Houstonians love to tell the tale about Richard Schill having a new Rolls Royce delivered a few days before one of the earlier Oktoberfest Round Top Antiques Fairs just so he could drive around the town square and direct visitors to the show. There he was, costumed in his red Western-style suit with his hat brim fastened to the crown like an Australian bush hat – except the fastener was a 10 carat diamond stick pin.

It has been a challenge – and a great pleasure – to sponsor, manage, produce and host this incredible country show for thirty years. Taking the risks, setting the standards of excellence in country shows and the loyalty found in both patrons and dealers has made every minute of time and every penny of every dollar invested worth it.

During the first two shows, before my own 1854 farm house was restored and could be occupied, I would get up at 5 a.m. on Friday morning and drive to Round Top. There, at 8, I would meet Rifle Association President Clarence Hinze and we would measure off the booths in the Hall to be ready for exhibitor setup starting at 9 a.m. Just as we share the same birthday, we shared this chore for many years together.

Today, it takes fifty-five people to prepare the grounds and buildings and ten days to set up the show. Work on the grounds, fight-

ing fire ants and improving ground conditions, continues throughout the year. Those fifty-five people don't include the dozens of food preparers and the Deputy Sheriffs who work tirelessly all weekend.

In our Houston office, one person spends each day all year answering calls, mail and e-mail with information on the show and helping people find their way to Round Top. Another handles all of the computer work from preparing advertising and press kits to maintaining the large patron mailing list to designing exhibitor name tags for each show. More than a week is spent just applying labels and preparing the mailing of show invitations.

I hope these pages will help explain why the Round Top Show is uniquely itself. It's always great for shopping, terrific people watching, a good excuse to go off your diet a little and a chance to walk in boots like you were born to.

Yours for Great Adventures in Antiquing,

– Emma Lee Turney

Acknowledgements

♦♦♦♦♦♦♦

It would be hard to say when I first started planning to write a book about The Round Top Antiques Fair because in this office, we are always "planning on writing about something."

Six years ago, I started bringing interior photographers Ogden Robertson and Blaine Hickey to Round Top to photograph exhibitors booths. It has been a continuing project ever since. Since Round Top is ninety miles out in the country, my thanks go to them as well as photographers Blair Pittman, Curtis McGee and Betty Tichich – each of whom have come to the Round Top show in rain or shine to help record the event for us. I also want to thank exhibitor Cynthia Anderson for sharing some of her photographs with us and *Antiques and the Arts Weekly* and *Antique Review* for allowing us to use photographs taken by Karla Klein Albertson when she was on assignment for them.

Three years ago, I mentioned the book to Beverly Harris, then Lifestyle Editor of the *Houston Chronicle* and she expressed an interest in working with me on it. Wasn't that a boost, especially since Beverly was born at Round Top and had interesting stories about the early days of the town? Beverly has brought a unique input to the book that took it far beyond the chronicle of the show that I originally had in mind. She and her cousin, Daniel Klar, provided stories and photographs from their family album. Thank you, Beverly, for sharing your editorial skills, your patience, various lunches here and there, and for taking such a personal interest in something so dear to me.

Madeleine McDermott Hamm, Home Design Editor for the *Houston Chronicle* is a special talent. Her writing style – whether on something as structured as a Home Tour, ASID award-winning design or the season at High Point – always reflects an enthusiasm that sounds as if it were the most important story she's ever written. Madeleine is never at a loss for new words. Her interest in antiques shows, especially the Round Top Antiques Fair, both as an observer and as a collector – has been a great contribution to the collecting public. She has shown, time and again, how country pieces can be used in decorating styles both in town and in the countryside.

Madeleine has been writing about the Round Top Antiques Fair from its early beginnings. She has seen it grow and maintain a consistency found in few shows. She is a good friend to us all and her comments in this book speak for her continuing interest.

Thanks to the *Houston Chronicle* for allowing us to publish the sketches of Round Top by Charles Pfister that appeared in 1969 in the first story on the Antiques Fair.

And for their help along the way, thanks go to Gloria Jaster Hickey, Director of Winedale Historical Center, A Division of the Center for American History, University of Texas at Austin, Texas, for her assistance on behalf of Winedale. And, to Barry Moore, FAIA, and Jo Ann Moss Ayres, for their assistance on behalf of Texas Pioneer Arts Foundation, the Administrator of Henkel Square. And for their help on researching Round Top history, thanks to Georgia Etzel Tubbs and Herb Diers.

◆ ◆ ◆ ◆ ◆ ◆ ◆

Thanks to Arthur F. Stokes and Mario Erwin for the photographs of Festival Institute and, of course, to James Dick, for his interest in this book and for always being so helpful and encouraging.

Thank you, too, to Connie Going of C.Going Publishing Company, Newport, Rhode Island. As my first partner in producing shows, Connie shared her experience not only as a preservationist but also her advertising background. She showed me how to write press releases and how to get targeted publicity. I am especially grateful to her for finding Book Production Coordinator Susan McNally and Graphic Designer Matthew Monk, who both found it interesting that there is a historical side to this book.

Finally, my right hand for nearly seventeen years has been Barbara Tungate. A friend for some thirty years, Barbara joined our office as the Editor of Southwest Antiques News. She brought her experience as everything from a proofreader to a copywriter and public relations account executive for major Houston advertising agencies. As a lifelong art collector, it was easy for her to understand the thinking of the collector. Blessed with a good eye and an interest in many things, she has also been an antiques dealer and knows that side as well. Like others who work with us, she wears many hats. There's one for computer work, another for writing ad campaigns and press releases, another for overseeing the mailing list, yet another for managing our Carmine venue. Just listening to me for six years as I talked about this book should be enough to add a halo to her hat rack.

Emma Lee Turney
Houston, Texas
January 1, 1998

◆ ◆ ◆ ◆ ◆ ◆ ◆

Denim
and
Diamonds

◆◆◆◆◆◆◆◆

◆◆◆◆◆◆◆

A very rare early 19th century table of walnut, poplar and cherry from
the rural area of the Georgia, Tennessee, Alabama corner of the Southeast.
Shown by Kathleen Vance and Mark Amis, Greenville, Virginia.
Photo, Hickey/Robertson

Football and sporting collectibles,
Julie Harris, Kansas City, Kansas. Photo, Hickey/Robertson

CHAPTER ONE

Discovering Round Top – Over and Over, Again

◆ ◆ ◆ ◆ ◆ ◆ ◆

IN JUST BEING ITSELF between exuberant cultural events, tiny Round Top, Texas, population eighty-one, almost re-creates its past. For the visitor, there is no difficulty imagining what the settlers saw – some of the earliest buildings still stand. Quite near, there are no buildings at all, only slightly rolling land with venerable woods forming a transition between East Texas soaring pines and West Texas tumble weeds.

In the 1930s, two young brothers, Dan and Wesley Klar, held that past in their hands. They had been exploring the cedar brakes behind their Grandmother Cecelia Wagner Graf's farmland when they spotted an ancient lone oak. They might have walked on by, but the thing had an intriguing hole about six feet up where a limb had rotted and fallen off. The hole was rimmed with opossum hairs. In their minds, this meant a possible trophy. Running to the barn for an ax and matches, the boys had their plan – they would smoke the creature out and chase it down.

Back at the site, they easily hacked through a thin section of sapwood. But on a particular stroke, the blade contacted something that made sparks fly. Possums were common; treasures were not. Old wood crumbled and out

Daniel W. Klar, a semi-retired civil engineer in Colusa, California, framed this portion of the Indian arrowheads and tools he and his brother uncovered in Round Top decades ago. Recently he donated the find to the Round Top Historical Society. Photo, Curtis McGee

spilled a huge cache of Indian arrowheads and tools. In that moment, Comanche artisans of the previous century returned in spirit to touch two awestruck boys.

Round Top continues to awaken its past. Each May there is a meeting of old-timers who attended the "old school" and the "new school," neither of which exists anymore. How the memories fly. In their day, before telephones were common, it was customary and sensible during terrible weather for a student to stay the night at the nearest relative or friend's house. Trusting parents didn't even worry about the missing child, according to one of the former students. The few remaining of that same generation remember the smell of kerosene lamps, homemade soap and lighted candles on fresh-cut cedar Christmas trees (a bucket of water stood by).

And when these elders recall tales their own grandparents told, they awaken the days of the early German settlers who built Round Top on a foundation of farming, woodworking, shop keeping, religion and scholarship.

Regarding the latter, the Rev. J. Adam Neuthard (1861-1902) established a boarding school. Master of French, German, Latin, Greek and Hebrew, he taught languages, geometry, algebra and music. And, yes, Round Top also had a banker, a lawyer, a cigar maker and a saloonkeeper.

Many of the old stories are told with accents. German can still be heard in Round Top. Along with the language, there remains a vestige of the Germanic outlook on life. It goes back to the original reasons their ancestors came to Texas: restrictive politics and rigidly controlled economy, among others. They deter-

Karen Murray and Shelby Gregory from Arrow Rock , Missouri,
always have a booth filled with stacks and stacks of good country furniture.
Photo, Hickey/Robertson

mined to leave for a place where they could utter their own opinions and make their own choices.

People came from

very long distances indeed...

In choosing her show site thirty years ago, Emma Lee had history on her side because there had been a steady trickle of people discovering the area from the time it was a wilderness.

European explorers may have traversed its rolling land as far back as the 1500s. Indians camped near its fresh water creeks and sampled the fruits of black haw trees and warriors chipped arrowheads out of its flint rocks. They felt the land was theirs by the grace of the Great Spirit. However, in "civilized" records, it was part of Mexico and therefore belonged to Spain until Mexico won its independence.

At that point Texas saw an influx of Anglo-American frontiersmen. The Mexican govern-ment actually encouraged them to form small colonies. But those early Texans didn't always behave according to regulations. While their bosses tried to rule from distant Mexico City, settlers often preferred America for culture, religion and trade. It was familiar and handy. Furthermore, Americans conveniently spoke English.

Already armed, the pioneers used Indian skirmishes as an excuse to form militias. Many political struggles with Mexican leaders inevitably set the stage for a series of battles (Remember the Alamo!) which eventually won Texas its independence. A few years later, in 1845, the Republic of Texas officially became the twenty-eighth state of the Union.

By that time another doggedly independent contingent was arriving. These were Germans who were so frustrated with their own overbearing rulers and lopsided economics that they allowed themselves to be lured by promis-es of freedom and prosperous farming in the

new land. Other nationalities, Czechoslovakians, Poles, Moravians, were represented, but Germans made up the largest contingent of immigrants to Texas at that time.

They came by tempestuous, crowded voyages, experiencing famine and thirst during the three months' passage. Some were buried at sea. Some were buried on land between their disembarkation point and their hoped-for settlement – disease, bitter cold, lack of supplies and Indian threats conspired against them.

Today many towns in Central Texas are testimony to the survivors. Round Top is one of them. Known variously as Jones Post Office and Townsend, the community eventually was named for the circular cupola on a house that served as an Indian lookout and landmark for the stagecoach. That, at least, is one version of the story.

Unlike those early citizens of Texas who rejected the ruling culture, Round Top Germans made it a point to show special respect for their new country – their liberty – by celebrating the American flag which itself represented hard-won independence.

Let Us a Parade Make

Round Top's Fourth of July Parade has been a social high point since 1851 and is the oldest such celebration West of the Mississippi. It has floats, it has costumes, and it has antique cars. It has bicycles and Texana Trail Riders; it has the Round Top Brass Band, politicians and bunting. It has a cannon, too, with only one misfortune recorded. On July 3, 1889, the cannon was being tested for the next day's festivities when it exploded. A metal fragment whooshed through the bowed legs of an official

without scratching him but severely wounded the next in line, according to one newspaper account.

If today's parade spectator, bathed in blistering heat but sustained by iced-down beverages, doesn't get a good view of a favorite float the first time around town hall square, he only needs to stand still. It will come around again – and again – with no loss of enthusiasm.

For many years, Independence Day with its parade, barbecue and family party (babies were bundled down safely under benches while adults danced to a community band's oom-pah-pah beat) was the main draw for visitors. How things have changed.

Newcomers to Round Top can expect to be welcomed politely. Many farms and ranches in the area have been purchased and developed by outsiders, city folks, who in good time are accepted by the community, especially if they demonstrate devotion for hard work. But it is interesting to note which of the business people appear to have been chosen by the discriminating town instead of the other way around.

The result of that selectivity is a cultural rush of classical music festivals, Shakespearean drama, folk art, gourmet food and the finest antiques from all over the country. The place can change overnight to a Mecca for seekers of life's refinements. So intense is the influx of visitors, including writers and photographers, that downtown Round Top, built around a square, has put up a traffic light and named its streets.

In April, city folks who have suffocated their wildflowers under concrete, also flock to Round Top and environs to marvel over the sight of highways and fields defined by washes of blues and reds. The little town announces its autumn with a startling staccato of acorns cracking down on tin roofs such as that of the old Rifle Hall.

Its own social activities include elaborate formal weddings, the events of three active churches, December's arrival of Santa on the square, a few dances, chicken fries, a lunch bunch that gathers monthly in someone's home, graduation ceremonies and fund-raisers by such as the DYD club – acronym for Do Your Duty, a directive that suits the character of citizens present and past.

When we say that Round Top is ninety miles from Houston, the nation's fourth largest city, we must be careful not to imply that it sits in the shadow of any metropolis. Or that it is even on a main highway. It is deep country complete with rural mail delivery, fire ants and longhorn cattle that stare at pickup trucks rumbling to somewhere else. Mid week, especially in the winter, most of the stores on the square are closed, with the exception of the Mercantile. Then Round Top becomes one of the quietest places on earth, not counting the occasional whoosh of a passing car or the squawk or an ill-tempered blue jay. And as night settles, an unbelievable number of stars watch over its eighty-one citizens and a few oil pumps.

◆ ◆ ◆ ◆ ◆ ◆ ◆

Great things shown by New York's Mario Pollo.
Photo, Hickey/Robertson

Jim Lord and Bobby Dent of the Comfort Common, Comfort, Texas, showed this very rare
Southern red cupboard. It is all original, peg and mortise construction with chamfered panels.
It originated in Georgia and is made of pine with original red paint. It dates from 1850-1860.
Photo, Hickey/Robertson

Privileges and Responsibilities

♦ ♦ ♦ ♦ ♦ ♦ ♦

From the *Houston Chronicle*, April 30, 1989

"On weekends she went barnstorming with her attorney father. There she was in a Stinson, swooping out of the clouds over Indian Territory and believing this was a perfectly normal family activity during the Dust Bowl days."

ADVERSITY STRUCK but barely left a dent in the early life of Emma Lee Turney. Her parents' marriage did not survive the Great Depression. When she was a year old, she was handed over to her mother's friends, the Turney family of Tulsa, Oklahoma. Suddenly she had four older siblings and they in turn had a little sister to dote on. Looking back on her childhood, she says, "I couldn't have been luckier. They were a haven of love and never ending adventure."

She recalls having every kind of pedal car imaginable. There were airplanes, fire engines and roadsters. "If only I had saved them – they are so collectible now!" She recalls donating a dozen of them to a scrap metal drive during World War II. "I also sacrificed a quart jar of Indian head pennies to be recycled for the war effort," she said. In addition to the avalanche of toys, she also had singing and dancing lessons, and at age twelve, learned to drive. By high school, she had her own navy blue two-door 1941 Chevy sedan. She owed that early bonanza to her dad's conviction that a car was not a luxury, but a necessity.

But there could be only so much cotton candy in a Depression economy where an ordinary bowl of soup earned solemn respect. Ballast in the Turney family was their deep commitment to help neighbors in need. In time Emma Lee realized she herself was an example of their altruism.

The Right Way

The family's guiding hand was mother Flora Turney, who was firm in her philosophy. She believed there was only one way to do anything: the right way. Emma Lee remembers, "She never put herself first. She was always giving, always overseeing huge meals, sometimes as many as twenty when friends were included. And in those days, out-of-work men often knocked at the back door for handouts. Mother Flora cooked for them, too, and treated them with such dignity," remembers Emma Lee.

Those animated and stimulating family dinners were an excuse to recall great experiences. Here the little sister learned that her new brothers and sisters had visited with Charles Lindbergh and photographed his monoplane,

17

Spirit of St. Louis, just before he took off for New York to begin his famous journey to Paris. They flew to Oklahoma City in their own plane to meet Amelia Earhart and they visited the Century of Progress Fair in Chicago. Emma Lee listened and soaked up the excitement, the fascination of having ideas and promptly acting upon them. If something was going on in the world, she soon learned, the Turneys urgently needed to be a part of it.

That philosophy prevailed during the darkness of a January night in 1936 when news came on the radio that King George V of England had died. Emma Lee was rousted out of bed to listen to a momentous broadcast. Also they felt she needed to be present at special memorial ceremonies for Will Rogers at Oologah, Oklahoma, near Claremore where the famous entertainer was born. The family had been friends of his pilot, Wiley Post, who perished with Rogers when they crashed at Point Barrow, Alaska.

Early in the 1930s, the family spent summers climbing Albuquerque's nearby mountains and traveling along the back roads of New Mexico just to soak up all the details. During a visit in Houston, Emma Lee's sister, Thelma Turney Myers, reminisced about a trip to Santa Fe in the 1930s when the family stayed at the pueblo/Spanish style La Fonda Hotel, located at the end of the Santa Fe Trail. Drovers were still escorting their livestock right through town – Thelma and Emma Lee watched through sidewalk-level windows of the hotel as cattle and horses clomped past. Emma Lee was too young to remember, but has visited the Santa Fe hotel since and marvels that today the restored heirloom has fourteen new luxury

A Martha Waldie, Dallas, Texas, booth with a couple of nice
Windsor chairs, and a good looking blue cupboard.
That's Stephen F. Austin to the right of the cupboard.
Austin led the original 300 colonists to Texas. Photo, Hickey/Robertson

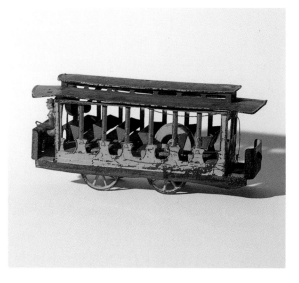

suites with no sacrifice to the sunset views from the Bell Tower and to the general old world ambiance.

Another destination was the Arkansas Ozarks to visit relatives. Enough Cherokee herself to have registered for voting rights, Emma Lee found it fascinating to walk near the White River in search for arrowheads and flints. "They were so plentiful, the local farmers would stack them, then dump them in the river to clear the fields for crops," she said.

Her curiosity stirred by all the sights, Emma Lee decided to become an archeologist. A bit later, she decided architecture was the way to go. At one point she wanted to be a movie photographer. Finally her romantic teen-age ambitions dissolved under the clear gaze of her Dad.

"He told me – adamantly – that if I would go to Business College, he would send me any place in the world for my advanced education."

Not quite ready to take on the world, she chose Houston because two brothers and a sister already lived there. Then, at her graduation, her Dad handed her a surprise.

Anywhere You Want To Go

"Well, now that you are so smart," he said, "just go out and earn your living and take yourself anywhere you want to go."

Apparently he had changed his mind about sending her to college. For whatever reason and he did not elaborate, he left no doubt that he was cutting her loose from family handouts. It seemed abrupt, even hurtful, to Emma Lee. Did her wonderful foster family no longer care for her? She gave that dramatic possibility a lot of thought.

Finally she understood it couldn't be so. She came to realize that she had received the best of all gifts – her independence.

20

The Cherokee Check

Emma Lee recalls:

My birthmother Ann had spent months at the records offices in Muskogee and Tahlequah, Oklahoma, sifting through files of names and records to prove that she was the great-granddaughter of a Cherokee who walked the Trail of Tears. That dreadful forced migration from Georgia, Tennessee and North Carolina to Oklahoma, a virtually uninhabited barren land, took countless lives and dealt misery to the survivors.

Under President John F. Kennedy's administration, Congress awarded $9 Million to the descendents. Proving kinship was a real chore because many Cherokees changed their names after Oklahoma's Indian registration in the early 1900s. But Ann persevered and finally established her rights.

We anticipated the arrival of "the check" with great expectations. Would we be able to retire? Take unlimited vacations?

I shall never forget the day my mother called to tell me "the check" had arrived. She said it was the most beautiful she had ever seen. It pictured the head of a grand Indian chief in full colorful regalia. She told me, "I want you to see this beautiful check, but send it back – I'll send you my own check for half the amount which I want to share with you."

"The check" finally arrived. Indeed it was beautiful. Inside the envelope was also Ann's personal check for my half. It was for eighteen dollars.

It seems the promised $9 million had dwindled away in administrative costs within the Indian Nation and for lawyer fees.

There went our daydreams! We had a good laugh at ourselves. But at least we had established our part in history and we are proud of our heritage to this day. No retirement, few vacations, and I am still working for a living.

How did they do that? How did the American Indians of the Southwest get
those intricate geometric and ribbon designs positioned on the round?
Prehistoric American Indian pottery left to right, olla, pitcher and round bowl.
Turney collection. Photo Betty Tichich

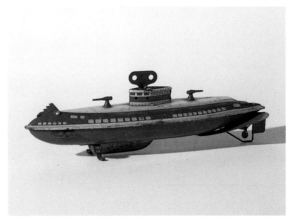

Furthermore, it came wrapped in the Turney brand of can-do, experimental spirit, and tied with a voluminous ribbon of propriety and self-confidence. Not bad for a girl who was about to get her first job.

Emma Lee was hired by a frame studio and trained as a gilder in the meticulous European style. Her duty? She was required to gold leaf handmade frames. Very young and full of energy, she had a steady hand, not to mention talent. But to do the same thing every-day? All day long? Was this the destiny of a girl who had soared the Oklahoma skies in a Stinson?

Fortunately, greater adventures were to come.

◆ ◆ ◆ ◆ ◆ ◆ ◆

*Julie Teichholz, Old Wicker Garden, Dallas, Texas, and a booth
filled with wicker, textiles and tramp art boxes. Photo, Hickey/Robertson*

An 1895 wooden gun trade sign from Northern Pennsylvania
and a booth filled with treasures, Don Orwig, Corunna, Indiana. Photo,
Hickey/Robertson

CHAPTER THREE

Where No Dust Cloth Has Been

♦♦♦♦♦♦♦

NOTHING STIRS THE SOUL of an antiques buff like original dust. The incredible find. Only the folks who uncover dinosaur bones can compare in excitability.

In her early twenties, Emma Lee Turney and a few of her friends indulged in antiques scouting as their Saturday hobby. It was a delightful way to socialize. They bought many splendid items, most of which they didn't really need. Logically, the next step was to sell those same items at a profit. The bug had bitten.

The Antiquers Dream, A Dusty Old Attic!

One day a friend declared she knew of an old store in the small town of Colmesneil, Texas, which might yield some treasures. Off they flew in a pickup truck.

"We found this wonderful store run by a gentleman in a blue serge suit – Mr. Meadows was relaxing by a pot-bellied stove," said Emma Lee. She believes he also was the town postman and possibly held other crucial titles.

"My friend asked if we could go upstairs to see what he had in storage. He not only agreed but let us know he wouldn't mind getting rid of it all."

What a find! Under the dust lay turn-of-the-century shoes, mannequins, elegant old store fixtures and hundreds of early hand blown bottles, some with gold labels, some with medicinal products still intact. An inspiration came to the two young women; suddenly they had a vision of Westbury Square, at that time Houston's first deliberately quaint shopping center, which was all the rage. They wondered, wouldn't some of the shop owners there find these showcases irresistible?

It took no time to arrange a price. "The gentleman charged from a nickel to twenty-five cents for the bottles, and from three dollars for the small cases to six dollars for the large ones," said Emma Lee. The same country store type fixtures today sell for $1,000 to $2,000 a piece. Apparently he believed they were doing him a big favor. With their truck filled to capacity, they promised to return next weekend and empty the attic.

Now We're Talking Business

Sure enough, some of the shopkeepers at Westbury felt enriched by their find, and paid a price that substantially increased the entrepreneurs' capital. This business was getting serious! With her enthusiasm on high, it was a natural progression for Emma Lee to continue by becoming an antiques dealer, a shopkeeper and to start managing and producing shows, initially with a friend and later on her own.

The first show was near Tarkington Prairie in Liberty County, forty miles north of Houston, on a historical site owned by her former partner. Dubious friends tried to convince them that very few people would bother to drive the distance. That attitude only challenged them. Defiantly, they put in motion a publicity and advertising campaign in regional and national publications, including the "Things To Do" column in *Life*, premier magazine of the 1960s. Behold, the effort lured 6,000 shoppers to the show in one day.

A cupboard filled with Bennington and Rockingham ware.
Photo, Hickey/Robertson

Incredible folk art shellwork mirror in Suzan Dentry's booth,
Golden, Colorado. Photo, Hickey/Robertson

Managing and Producing Her Own

The overwhelming success at Tarkington Prairie guided Emma Lee to a viable business of her own. She chose a name for her company: "Antiques Productions." Houston, cities in South Texas, and New Orleans accepted her style of business, which was inviting dealers known for fine quality antiques to set up booths under a single roof, then supporting the combined effort with targeted advertising and publicity. A bonus was her contagious enthusiasm. As it turned out, each show was more successful than the last.

Without a doubt, Emma Lee had chosen her life's work. It was a Turney kind of career involving people, places and things. It promised an adventure around every corner, but most important to Emma Lee was the enormous potential. It was dawning on her that she could provide both a forum and a marketplace to introduce the public to the joys of collecting.

Preserving Heritage – with a Passion

Early in her career in the 1960s as an antiques dealer, Emma Lee realized that nothing was being done to preserve the heritage and culture of rural America and that became her passion. All the right ingredients were readily available from the Midwest to Maine and especially in the Maryland and Pennsylvania countryside to which she was drawn. A friendship with the late Marcia Ray, Editor in Chief of Spinning Wheel magazine, opened doors throughout those two states to Turney and her partner. Soon they were scouring the countryside, bringing to Texas truckloads of country benches, decorated stoneware, white stoneware, slipware, Windsor chairs, John Bell pots, six-board blanket chests, country store advertising pieces – and even the bench for making mouse traps that had come from the Francis Scott Key farm in Maryland. They found so many beautiful quilts, coverlets and textiles that the finds lost their value and were ahead of their time for

Texas collectors. It was these fruitful trips that helped stir the wish among Texas collectors to re-create the lifestyle of rural America in their own homes, whether in the country or city.

Her finds were keyed to dealers and decorators. These were happy, productive days that allowed her to shut her shop doors for weeks at a time and venture forth to the antiquers' frontiers. Like all frontiers, however, there were always new horizons. By the early 1970s, she felt the lure of foreign markets. Her next destination she decided would have to be England.

And Now to England

She began asking questions. "This will be easy for you," offered one expert, Marty Adler. He gave her names of a shipper, courier, dealers in London and the English countryside. Some of the dealers were already familiar names because they had contacted Emma Lee, hoping she could spare them space in one of her shows.

Emma Lee wrote letters, made appointments. Then away she went. The next two weeks would be a maelstrom of activity, best epitomized by the courier Maggie Brown who rarely slowed her vehicle below seventy miles per hour. "Not only that, I couldn't shake the sinking feeling that we were tearing down the wrong side of the road," said Emma Lee.

Maggie, who had performed secretarial duties for royalty, knew all the little hidden shops as well as the major ones. She delighted in showing off the just-completed retail shops housed in the stables at Woburn, then turning down a lane (at top speed) to find a place where tourists had never been.

Many of Emma Lee's purchases were functional goods such as rural tables and chairs created in the early nineteenth century, along with exquisite Chinese export, Staffordshire and wonderful trade signs. While she was buying, Maggie, trained in these matters, handled the import/export documents for shipping. Later the shipper had a lorry pick up the purchases for placement in twenty-foot containers. Six weeks later they would ply their way up the Houston Ship Channel.

In her free time, Emma Lee missed none of the tourist attractions but got real satisfaction from gathering information in her chosen field. She attended the annual Antiques Fair at Grosvenor House and various studies at the Victoria and Albert Museum.

"I always tried to study a course in something I didn't know a thing about, such as Japanese woodblock prints, then learn more about a familiar subject, such as the miniature theatres which I collected." she said.

Then there was the lecture on a Leonardo de Vinci text. It was a feeling of exhilaration just to be in the presence of such a valued piece of history. However, the presentation turned out to be considerably less educational than Emma Lee had hoped – only after she was seated and the doors closed did she realize that the lecture was entirely in Italian. She barely understood a word.

Conquering Canada

She took many more trips to England between 1971 and 1973 on behalf of her decorator and dealer clients. One year she went five times. Meanwhile, she also discovered a relatively untapped antiques market in beautiful provincial areas of Canada. Incredibly, her driver for these trips was a former Indianapolis speed racer.

In Canada, she found old barns stuffed with rural-style stretcher-based tables, chairs, cupboards and block front wardrobes with scalloped bases. The colors tended toward rich teal, burgundy, delicate salmon and yellow.

"Some people like to think Canadian rural furniture is the same as New England's," said

Emma Lee, "but I can spot a Canadian piece across a crowded show floor. It has a special, charming look. The wood is cut thicker for tabletops and cupboards and the designs reflect what the Canadians called Louis XV style of embellishment."

In contrast to the sophistication of London and surroundings and the frenzy of importing was the lure of Round Top. In the late 1960s Emma Lee bought five early Texas houses. She restored and sold one, and now in 1975, wanted to go back and restore the rest. It would make sense, she decided, to live there, roughly half way between her Houston and Austin shows, closer to the San Antonio show and on site for her Round Top event.

Emma Lee's Pioneer Woman Act

Feeling in harmony with the spirits of brave pioneer women versus the wilderness, Emma Lee set up housekeeping in her five-room farm-house. Little did it matter that there were cracks between the floorboards. She would cover them with her Oriental and Navajo rugs. She would bring in electricity and plumbing as concessions to contemporary living, but planned to harvest her own vegetables and graciously offer weekend guests the overflow of her bounty. She saw herself sitting on the porch listening to a gentle breeze ruffling the grasses and leaves in harmony with birdsong and those many other unidentifiable sounds of nature. She would meditate on all the fine improvements that could be made on her five acres.

Meanwhile, she opened an antiques shop in her country Greek revival house and set up an office in her favorite purchase, a one-room immigrant cottage which is now located at Frances and Bill Harris' Heart of My Heart Ranch Bed and Breakfast Inn.

Anybody see my book on being a Pioneer Woman?

The saga of Emma Lee-In-The-Country lasted for three years, no more.

As it turned out, her modern conveniences were no match for what Texans call a blue norther, an urgent wind straight from the Arctic that in a matter of minutes can drop normally mild temperatures by fifty degrees or so. A famous Texas tall tale insists that once a horse, trying to outrun a norther, galloped desperately toward the stable. His head and forelegs made it but the parts that followed did not, freezing solid in mid stride.

The day Emma Lee looked out the window and saw glistening icicles all along her porch and ice-coated trees too stiff to bend, she gathered logs which she herself had chopped to custom fit the wood cook stove and extra small fireplace. The heat they put out made little impression. While the plumbing froze, she set her electric heaters on high. No good. The way wind knifed through them, the thin walls of her house could as well have been gauze. Her collector rugs didn't even pretend to cover the entire floor, so every crack became a vent for compressed frigid drafts. Emma Lee grabbed an extension cord, attached it to her electric blanket and bundled up. Thus tethered, she could only roam as far as the entry hall where it was so cold that her breath came out as frost.

The bone-chilling episode coincided with a revelation: somehow Emma Lee had misplaced the instructions for becoming a pioneer woman. She decided to return to Houston where she could function better in the business of show management, saving the enjoyment of nineteenth century houses for entertaining on long weekends.

Back among the skyscrapers, she was surprised to discover that she no longer needed to have invitations hand-addressed for her lengthy mailing lists. Avery labels, along with other office conveniences, had been invented in her absence. For three years she had been driving all the way to Brenham, twenty miles away, to conduct simple business procedures, such as copying materials. In Houston, her work was faster, simpler, less stressful. True, no one waved to her in friendly country greeting each day, but that's life in the big city.

In 1990, she finally let go of the old house and its five acres, selling it to her good friend Roland Nester whom, with his sister Mary Stanhope, turned it into the quaint Briarfield Bed & Breakfast.

Better judgment may have amended her ambitions as a pioneer, but she did accomplish something special during those three years. Solitude and isolation were ideal for writing her first book gleaned from all her buying trips and research. The result was "Antiques Business as a Lifestyle," published in 1978 and sold in the United States and five foreign countries. This was the first book on how to become an antiques dealer and open a shop. It also detailed facts about importing and included an extensive source and resource directory listing services, antiques markets and dealers.

At the same time, her shows for the public were attracting crowds in San Antonio, Austin and Houston, and what was to become the really big show in Round Top was growing. Antiques hunters in Texas, caught up in the American rural lifestyle, couldn't get enough of country furnishings and accessories.

Oklahoma's little girl who found a dream family was now to achieve her own measure of success.

◆ ◆ ◆ ◆ ◆ ◆ ◆

A six-board blanket chest with scalloped base in original red paint.
And, look at that game board in front, it's all original.
Rick and Dwan Mabrey, Raleigh, North Carolina.
Photo, Hickey/Robertson

CHAPTER FOUR

Home Sweet Second Home

◆◆◆◆◆◆◆

DURING THE 1960S AND 1970S, the Washington County area (near Round Top) became known as the "Brenham/Connecticut area." New money had been made in Houston. Second homes, weekend retreats, horse farms and vast ranches testified to the fortunes of oil barons, insurance moguls and some international financiers.

In decorating their country places, wives of the well-to-do often turned to the safe, established styles of England and New England. Then, when the houses were fully embellished with formal and colonial antiques, fine china and silver, they begged to be admired.

Invitations blossomed. Sumptuous dinners, elegant guests, international figures, even heads of State enlivened many a weekend and provided gushing newspaper society editors with a steady stream of bold-faced names. In some cases those names arrived by private planes, which landed on their hosts' runways. It was a Texas version of "Golden Age of the Country House," in which Christopher Sykes chronicled the English weekend holidays during the late nineteenth century.

The round twig table came from the area between Greenville and Anderson, South Carolina
and was made by Washington Smith, an African-American well known in that area
for his unusual twig-work. The swags around the bottom and circular top are typical of his work.
Made in the first half of this century the piece still retains its original finish.
Kathleen Vance and Mark Amis, Greenville, Virginia. Photo, Hickey/Robertson

Whoa! Back Up

But something was missing. Affluent Texans were so busy emulating the eastern establishment that they overlooked their own heritage.

Enter the preservationists – specifically three dynamic women from Houston: Miss Ima Hogg, a founder of the Houston Symphony, Hazel Ledbetter and Faith Bybee. They and their followers, life-long friends who were also interested in collecting fine antiques and in finding their place in the Texas countryside, created a stir, an awakening to the great values at hand.

Undisputed leader of the group was the daughter of Texas Governor James S. Hogg (1851-1906). It is true, he named his little girl Ima, and that has been the subject of many a snicker. However, her name was a mere pebble to step over in face of the boulder that was Miss Ima. She exuded such graciousness, authority, charm and wit that she almost always got what she wanted.

Among other things, she wanted antiques. She was accustomed to finery and had no use for collecting merely for the sake of owning things. Hers was a loftier pursuit: She saw a need to preserve America's finest early furniture before it vanished. She helped design her own home with the idea, despite opposition from her River Oaks neighbors, that it would eventually become a museum. Thus, today, the lovely grounds (annually on Houston's Azalea Trail), twenty-two rooms and rare contents of the mansion Bayou Bend are now part of the Houston Museum of Fine Arts. Even the nation benefited from her refined taste. She served on the board of directors with Jacqueline Kennedy for restoration of the White House interior.

In another phase of her quest for excellence, she bought historic Stagecoach Inn at Winedale, Texas, from her friend Hazel Ledbetter who had acquired the property from the descendents of the Joseph Wagner family. The 190-acre complex is just down the road from Round Top and at that time was in desperate need of mending. Miss Ima, a purist, saw to it that every detail of the inn, down to the square nails and restoration of its original stenciling was authentic to its era. A friend recalls that the project gave Miss Ima a lift from a temporary depression caused by her rift with Bayou Bend neighbors. M. Wayne Bell, FAIA, professor of architecture at the University of Texas in Austin, was in charge of the Winedale restoration.

While that was going on, Miss Ima discovered and was captivated by Round Top. Her fascination with German workmanship probably began when she was a girl studying piano abroad under the tutelage of Berlin and Viennese masters. Now she found another antiquity in bad shape – the old Johann Traugott Wandke organ (dedicated in 1867) at Bethlehem Lutheran Church. She donated funds for its renovation and to the joy of locals, played the hand-built cedar instrument at its reawakening.

Active interest in Round Top by the three influential women from Houston was highly contagious. Competition was on for city folks to acquire property, original buildings, early Texas furniture and whatever wasn't nailed down.

What Did We Do with *Grossvater's* Bench?
Round Top citizens weren't always sure what to make of the commotion. However, they certainly were alerted to the fact that the furniture they had been living with nonchalantly, pieces handcrafted by their grandfathers and handed down by their parents, was worth much more than mere family sentiment. They were reminded now – with some of the wares doing rough duty in barns and stables – that their pre-

The partially hidden Chinese Chippendale style garden bench
and chair are exquisite examples of popular period garden furniture.
Margaret Shanks, Brenham, Texas. Photo, Hickey/Robertson

Dallas, Texas, antiques dealer Mary Cone's architectural windows
now reside in the collection of Colorado dealers, Nan and David Pirnack.

decessors had come from the old country with many valuable skills.

Johann Traugott Wandke, for instance, who was also a master of medicinal herbs, had the intricate plans for a pipe organ in his pocket when he crossed the ocean aboard the sailboat "Weser" in 1855. He built parts for seven of them for various towns in his little stone loft/workshop, which stands near enough to the Bethlehem Lutheran Church to feel the instrument's reverberations. Eventually weeds choked the little building and a family of rattlesnakes lived under the worn floor until its rescue and restoration. The historical stone building has been expertly restored by Houstonian Sandy Reed and houses the Herb Haus.

The actual pipe organs, three of which are still in playing condition, according to Wandke's descendent, Henry Pochmann of Dallas, were assembled within each church.

Lore has it that in Round Top, Wandke struck a note on another instrument at home, then, humming the tone, rushed for the nearby church to tune the new organ. If a passing neighbor greeted him, he merely stared and hummed in reply, no matter how high the pitch.

Others came with samples of their work, such as velvety wooden sewing boxes with tiny compartments, each covered with a curved lid that fit precisely and could be lifted by a miniature porcelain knob. These were the "final exams" that master craftsmen demanded of their graduating apprentices. Once they settled in Round Top, they exercised their craftsmanship by making tables, chairs, benches, dressers, cabinets and freestanding wardrobes, among other items, for their homes.

They built Teutonic style houses and barns to remind them of a country and the relatives they had left behind and might never see again.

A perfect example is the graceful Conrad Schueddemagen home on Highway 237 just past the square. A private property now, the two-story structure was built by Carl Siegismund Bauer in 1852 to replicate his Saxony home. Mrs. John Nielson, widow of a Houston insurance executive, restored the native limestone building. Bauer also planned and directed the building of the white limestone church at a cost of $2,400.

City folks longing for a tranquil place in the country took notice of the recent stirrings and a buying frenzy began. The late 1950s and into the mid-1970s saw a stream of Houstonians waiting in line on weekends outside Schatte Real Estate in Round Top. Any mid-nineteenth century farm house, smokehouse, barn or ranch would do. They restored everything in sight. Discriminating Annie Schatte, who was said to evaluate her customers' intent by the make of automobile they drove and the shoes they wore, became quite well to do herself from the onslaught of sales.

Dust, Decay and a Ghost Haus

Not quite everything survived. In 1938 the ramshackle school/boarding house next to the church met its doom. The two and one-half story stone building was erected in 1865-66 for the scholar Rev. J. Adam Neuthard and his wife. Their eventual deaths left a terrible silence over the house because their eight heirs, whether for German stubbornness or sentiment, never reached a settlement and consequently never reckoned with a single item.

According to Leonie Rummel Weyand in her "History of Round Top" written in 1924, layer after layer of dust accumulated until details of the fine old furniture all but vanished. Charred wood remained in the fireplaces. The reverend's ecclesiastical robes and several of his suits still hung in the most delicate moth-eaten condition where he left them and in the kitchen, jars of jelly solidified into rock sugar. In the bedroom, the beds were still made; in the dining room, the table was set for four, with not a piece of silver or dinnerware disturbed.

A copper fish weathervane. Photo, Blair Pittman

Children who attended a three-room school next to the vine-covered decaying house were strictly warned to keep away from the property. Naturally, the youngsters decided it was haunted. Its ghostly, crumbling facade remained decade after decade until it was finally leveled in 1938.

If only the dismantlers had known that the three powerful women of Houston and their friends were about to march over the horizon, they might have spared the relic.

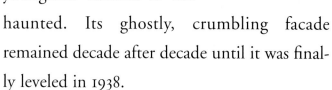

What's Past Is Not Passed

In contrast, most of the buildings in town are handsomely restored. Once considered quite modest by their owners, many now sport signs to identify their original families such as The Graf Haus and the Pochman House (originally spelled Pochmann). One showplace was known for a while as the old Bender place (Gustav Bender was proprietor of the Lone Star Saloon) which in its decline became rain-soaked throughout. Herb and Rose Diers of Houston bought it in 1983. A portion of the roof had been flipped back by a storm, windows were broken and some of the wood rotted.

"I could stand on the first floor, look through the ceiling and attic and see the sky," said Herb. As much a perfectionist as Miss Ima and one who loves research, he studied old photos and records of the unusual two-story house, which had been sitting unoccupied for fourteen years. Meticulously he restored its original design as built by William J. H. Umland in 1871. Its architecture moves toward high Victorian with references to other styles – hardly the usual German dogtrot cottage. Tourists with cameras seem drawn to the restoration, but sometimes could use discretion about proximity. It is, after all, a private residence.

Paisley shawls, hooked rugs, textiles and trays.
Lynne M. Brody, Georgetown, Texas. Photo Hickey/Robertson

Frankfort, Ohio's, Kay and Bill Puchstein and
a booth of very early furniture and one of those dapple hobby horses
that Texans like so much. Photo, Hickey/Robertson

Henkel Square

Faith Bybee with her husband Charles, a Houston banker, created Texas Pioneer Arts Foundation and Henkel Square by moving several historic buildings and a major collection of Texas pioneer furnishings and decorative arts to downtown Round Top. Before her death, her collection of Colonial American furniture and decorative arts was installed in a new wing of the Dallas Museum of Art. Recently, the Foundation sponsored the newly formed Round Top Arts Festival, a juried event for visual arts.

Georgia Etzel Tubbs

Local families have long since emptied smokehouses and butchering barns of any valuable handcrafted pieces. With the formation of the Round Top Area Historical Society Inc., spearheaded by Georgia Etzel Tubbs, the community has made a concentrated effort to house memorabilia, photos and printed material, much of it donated through the generosity of the original families. On property and in a small building deeded to Round Top by Lillian Kroll Thomas and Ruby Kroll in 1993, the mini-museum across the street from the bank on Highway 237 even houses a bit of pioneer furniture. Most of the early pieces, however, are in the hands of Texas collectors and other museums.

Winedale Inn

The legacy of Miss Ima, who died at age ninety-three because of an auto accident in London, was her donation of the Winedale Historical Center to the University of Texas. According to her wish, the UT English department sponsors a festival of Shakespeare's plays there in a restored barn. Her friend Dr. James B. Ayres,

creator and the original director of the program coaxes his students and some local citizens to raise the Bard's work to a new level of enthusiasm. Consequently, there are Round Top youths who have grown up with equal allegiance to the 4H Club and Shakespeare.

Institute at Festival Hill

And down Highway 237, a short distance northeast from Round Top's square, nestles the amazing Institute at Festival Hill. Its 200-acre campus is dominated by an imposing 1,200-seat Festival Performance Center. From outside, it delights the eye with its look of a massive Russian-Victorian concert hall with classic Palladian details. The year-round Festival Institute, founded by world-renowned pianist and wellspring of energy, James Dick, offers study with master musicians and public

performances. Ticket-holders like to picnic on the picturesque grounds in the shadow of the chapel spire and ancient live oaks and hike along its trails through woods, along lakes and across stone bridges. They may come for the day or spend the night in accommodations on campus or at a nearby bed-and-breakfast inn. Other attractions at Festival Hill are Herb Days workshops and tours of the gardens conducted by herbalist and author Madalene Hill and daughter, Chef Gwen Barclay.

Right Time for the Right Kind of Show

Thirty years ago, when Emma Lee Turney produced her first Round Top Antiques Fair, she actually envisioned today's cultural and fine arts activities. In each area of interest – restoration, antiques, classical music, advanced collecting – the leaders were at hand and the community of Round Top was the focus of their energy. She

Pennsylvania and Ohio coverlets. Photo Hickey/Robertson

A wide range of quilt patterns and styles.
Photo, Hickey/Robertson

knew that the timing for her show was exactly right.

Perhaps it was an insight owed to the days when she was an eight-year-old walking the corn rows in search of arrowheads and flints, much like those in the pastures of Round Top. She had an instinct for collecting objects of inherent value.

If she could bring together some of the nation's top dealers of fine American antiques, bring them to a place that cradled its own pioneer work, wouldn't collectors take notice? She was certain it would happen.

Emma Lee's method of turning a dream into action is backed by years of experience and legal pad lists of things-to-do. If she acts on a whim – and sometimes she does – it comes attached to a chain of logic. Thirty years ago, Round Top regarded her as just another one of those ambitious women from Houston. Today her effort is one of the reasons tiny Round Top is known as an important art town, being especially revered by antiques dealers and collectors throughout the country.

◆ ◆ ◆ ◆ ◆ ◆ ◆

Ann Hundley, Katy, Texas. Photo, Hickey/Robertson

CHAPTER FIVE

The Little Country Show and How It Grew

◆ ◆ ◆ ◆ ◆ ◆ ◆

As an antiques dealer, Emma Lee already knew one of the three Ladies From Houston. One day, a beautiful leather-bound *Bible,* published in Pennsylvania in the eighteenth century, caught Miss Ima's eye. She bought it from Emma Lee and placed it in the Winedale Historical Center. Later, there were other finds for Miss Ima from Emma Lee's Pennsylvania and Maryland trips.

Then in the spring of 1968 came a telephone invitation from Hazel Ledbetter to come to her farm at Round Top for dinner.

At the time, Hazel was well ensconced in Round Top. Her inventory included the Winedale Inn (as it was called then), a couple of farms and several of the mid-nineteenth century houses and buildings that had been constructed by German settlers in and around the town. She also bought the row of buildings just off the town square from the Schwarz estate. And most visible was her attractive antiques shop managed by former Houston florist and antiques dealer John Shaw, now of Chappell Hill, Texas. Carloads of Junior Leaguers from Houston were drawn to the shop and were spreading the word.

"Hazel was an excellent orchestrator and rarely did anything without a purpose," said Emma Lee. "She was a fountain of knowledge of how to do and when to do it."

Hazel's direction was soon revealed. She asked Emma Lee to establish a good antiques show in Round Top so that, as she put it, "the public would quit peeking in our windows to see what we are doing up here."

Very likely, much of that curiosity had been stirred by daily columnist Marguerite Johnston's article in the Houston Post, in which she told how the Ladies from Houston were saving original buildings and houses at Round Top. The story, first of its kind on Round Top, traveled all the way to the Congressional Record and possibly saved even more gems from being replaced by the then-current fad of modern ranch houses. Author of "A Happy Worldly Abode," and "Houston, The Unknown City 1836-1946," Marguerite was Assistant Editor of the Post's editorial page at her retirement. She with husband Charles Barnes and family have been weekenders in Round Top since 1963. She watched firsthand as the quiet little town timidly ventured forth into larger society.

Emma Lee savored the logic of Hazel's suggestion. But bringing her show to new territory so distant from regular patrons would need extra incentive, she decided, and countered Hazel's proposal with one of her own.

"I'll do it," she told her hostess, "if you will open your house to the public for the weekend. And how about asking the Harvin Moores to show their restored houses?" Architect Moore and his wife, Elizabeth, were among the first Houstonians to take on restoration in Texas. Emma Lee knew that antiquers from the city would be lured irresistibly by an offer to walk through those doors. Furthermore, the rush to the country had brought about 2,000 Houston families to nearby ranches, farms and weekend retreats. Many of their restored homes still

A thirteen star flag. Photo, Blair Pittman

A gold and blue mariner's compass shown by Joyce and Guy Hutchison,
Barnesville, Georgia. Photo, Hickey/Robertson

wanted authentic furnishings and owners would not be adverse to seeing how Hazel and the Moores had handled their own decorating needs.

Hazel pondered briefly, weighing the invasion of privacy against her own desire for a prestigious antiques show in Round Top. The antiques won.

Time, Place, Date

First order of business for Emma Lee was to look at the available site, which was a short drive down the road toward Winedale. There it sat at her left, on rocky terrain dappled by what sunshine the 150-year-old live oaks allowed through their lichen-covered mossy branches.

Emma Lee describes her first impressions of the weathered Round Top Schuetzen Verein, now called the Rifle Association Hall, and surrounding field, where marksmanship competitions have been going on for years: "It was a marvelous country grange, with flaps let down on its sides for ventilation. It had a freestanding peaked roof and the high ceiling was hung with colorful red, white and blue streamers, remnants of the latest Fourth of July celebration. Over the bandstand was a display of early advertising by local merchants."

In the pressing heat of a mid-summer afternoon she inspected the empty building. It even smelled old. Several five-foot ventilation fans stood idle, and in one corner sat testimony to the opposite season, a cast-iron pot-bellied stove. In her mind's eye, she saw it taking up space for a booth, so it needed to be relocated for the show. It took six men to move the great weight out and then back.

Emma Lee was enthralled. She enjoyed a twinge of anxiety, the sort that accompanies excitement. "It was such an extreme rural setting for the kind of polished collectors and cultural leaders we had in mind." She trusted they would be intrigued – she hoped her list of loyal antiques dealers could locate the place – she wondered if the locals would look kindly upon the stampede of shoppers she intended to create.

On the other hand, if the rest of the locals were anything like Clarence Hinze, Emma Lee's plan had an easy go. Clarence, respected citizen of Round Top and president of the Rifle Association, welcomed her with a charming smile and a soft German accent. He escorted her throughout the facilities, weighing amenities against Emma Lee's requirements. A fall date was chosen. Emma Lee told him she would like to honor the local heritage by naming the event Oktoberfest, Round Top Antiques Fair. Soon genial Clarence shook her hand. The deal was done Round Top-style.

Conversation between Emma Lee and Clarence was so easy they uncovered the fact that they had the same birthday, September 27, and pondered the astrological interpretation that Libras are lovers of great tranquility, beauty and peacemaking. Later it would turn out that in Clarence's case, peacemaking was a demonstrable attribute.

As a consequence of the meeting, on the first weekend in October 1968, Highway 237 was ruled by pickup trucks. Twenty-two antiques dealers thundered toward Round Top on tires painfully strained by maximum loads. It was set-up day, the hours before the public arrives when dealers find their assigned spaces and arrange their goods.

Among the drivers cruising down the highway was Emma Lee in a red truck carrying a seven-foot pine wardrobe of Texas origin. She was transporting it as a favor for a dealer because, in this pre-van age, pickup beds simply didn't hold much.

"People kept waving at me all along the road," she recalls. "I thought everyone was being friendly; it was so encouraging." As she slowed down in the town of Hempstead, a fellow at a car dealership managed to communicate by pointing emphatically. She looked back – the wardrobe was leaning at a perilous sixty-degree angle. Considering her former speed, it no doubt had repeatedly threatened to take flight.

*A vivid red and white Drunkard's Path forms a background
for Tulsa, Oklahoma dealers Barbara and Charles Davis' collection of blue
and white stoneware. Photo, Blair Pittman*

Never Easy

That event and later episodes reinforce Emma Lee's observation: "It was never easy – and it never gets any easier."

At one of the early shows Emma Lee and Miss Ima were chatting outside when a perturbed young man on horseback charged up. Alcoholic vapors filled the air as he announced his plan to save his country, flag, honor and Round Top from their invasion. He threatened to remove his belt and whip the two women. Either that, he decided, or he would ride into the Hall and thrash the antiques. His horse was obediently negotiating the stairs when Libra-born peacemaker Clarence Hinze arrived on the scene. Reasoning in his mild-toned diplomatic manner, Clarence not only averted disaster but also apparently convinced the intrepid warrior to take on some distant windmills and never return.

Local Cheerleaders

Two genuine optimists about the show's future were the late Don Nagel, who served as Round Top's mayor for thirty years, and the late Ernst Emmerich, town marshal. Don owned the Phillips 66 station and Ernst, the Texaco station. As businessmen, they both saw the Antiques Fair as an economic draw for Round Top, not to mention a cultural awakening. Their friendship and cooperation in ironing out details each year kept Emma Lee's enthusiasm and energy in high gear.

The Show Grows On

So during the 1970s all expectations were met, including an increase in dealers. By changing the booth arrangements in the Hall, thirty-two of them could now squeeze in. In the mid-seventies, many Texas antiques dealers started going to New England auctions and markets to supplement the demand for Texas antiques with fine American pieces.

Fall colors in shades of orange, gold and brown.
Photo, Hickey/Robertson

Emma Lee says, "As the success and regional fame of the show grew, more and more good antiques dealers wanted to be a part of our success. And many antiques dealers were discovering our Texas pickers who were able to buy directly from their sources in the German communities near Round Top, Brenham, New Braunfels, San Marcos and on to Fredericksburg. Too, San Antonio was yielding many Spanish Colonial and ranch antiques.

"By the early 1980s, many dealers and collectors from distant places had heard the word about Round Top. The attendance at the show began to grow to exceptional numbers and our waiting list reached a ridiculous eighty plus."

Former House Beautiful Editor and now author of some seventeen books on country decorating, collecting and more, Mary Ellisor Emmerling had already discovered Round Top during frequent visits to the area with her friend, Houston interior designer Beverly Jacomini and her husband, Tommy. It was Mary who, with a simple statement, helped Emma Lee solve the dilemma of how to expand the show to accommodate most of the waiting list:

"Why don't you use a tent out back like they do in New England?"

In fact, Emma Lee knew that tents were acceptable up and down the East Coast for everything from high society weddings and receptions in Newport, Rhode Island, to markets of all kinds.

"My first reaction was, Texans will never go for that – they'll think I'm selling used cars – but after thinking about it for ten whole minutes, my decision was made – if I could find a really good tent man.

"How lucky I was because I found the best tent man in the country in David Henry of O'Henry Productions from Mt. Calm, Texas. Our first tent was a huge two hundred-foot yellow and white striped one that cast a strange, eerie orange glow over everything and everyone it housed. Bright colored trapunto quilts took on a washed out look, white stoneware turned

yellow to orange, blues and grays turned a sickly green and the people all looked a bit jaundiced. But we were able to add another eighty-eight dealers to our original thirty-two up front in the Rifle Hall. And the vertigo-inducing, color-altering tent didn't stop the dealers from selling to the tent walls or the buyers from staying in there to buy.

"We were quick to replace that early tent with a custom-made football-field-sized white one that now enables buyers to view everything in natural light, got rid of the vertigo and restored people to good health. David is our champion and he is there rain or shine, helping take care of us from start to finish."

New Friends in the Friendliest Show

Behind the scenes was a new camaraderie among exhibitors. Established dealers took on the role of hosts to new arrivals from out-of-state. There was much to talk about. "Among our first out-of-state exhibitors were Louisiana's

Wilhelmina 'Bill' Cook, who was an excellent addition with her South Louisiana cypress furniture and rural American pieces, and Santa Fe's Robert Nichols with fabulous country furniture and American Indian pottery," recalls Emma Lee. As the show grew in the eighties and nineties, a large contingent of top dealers from outside Texas was added to the show. Many Texas dealers were broadening their search for upcoming Round Tops because knowledgeable collectors and museums were snapping up regional antiques. More and more were venturing out of state to look for American rural and country pieces, "just for Round Top." The new contacts were good for everyone. And it worked in reverse. Having met and worked with these roving Texas dealers who talked about the unique Round Top show, several of the East Coast and Midwest dealers began to put temporary GTT signs on their doors – a reference to the early 1800s when

A lot of red in quilts and coverlets in this booth.
Photo, Hickey/Robertson

adventurers announced in writing or carving their departure from the United States. GTT was a widely recognized signal that meant "Gone to Texas."

A Hall and A Tent – Still Not Enough...

Even with expansion, the waiting list grew once again. Emma Lee bought acreage on Highway 237 across from Festival-Institute. This time she attempted to conquer her waiting list time with a cedar barn entrance and another large custom-made white tent. As the Antiques Annex, this would take care of the dealer overflow and also add a new format for established folk artists, the Round Top Folk Art Fair.

A Hall, Two Tents, Two Sites – Still Not Enough...

The waiting list grew again. So, at the invitation of Berry Etzel and the members of the Carmine Dance Hall, a third site was added in the early 1990s. Because Carmine is the turn-off point to Round Top, it often is the starting line for collectors. What they find is another very old but air-conditioned dance hall filled with dealers from Maine, Pennsylvania, New York, New Mexico, Kentucky, Ohio and Maryland as well as Texas. With three locations to cover, collectors are in for a long foot-pounding weekend of fun and shopping. The members of the halls at Round Top and Carmine benefit by cooking barbecue all weekend long. The Round Top-Carmine 4H Club projects benefit by selling plants in front of the Rifle Hall. And the Round Top Youth Livestock Show Fund benefits from the proceeds of barbecue their group serves at the Antiques Annex and Folk Art Fair site.

Now in one sweep, visitors can descend on three locations and just hope the back seats and trunks of their autos and vans can accommodate all their finds.

◆◆◆◆◆◆◆

A collection of Milagros. Jan Hutchison, Pass Christian,
Mississippi. Photo, Hickey/Robertson

CHAPTER SIX

The Dealers and Some Fond Memories

◆ ◆ ◆ ◆ ◆ ◆ ◆

DEALERS OF ANTIQUES come in all shapes, sizes and personalities. Some are fresh and innocent, some wrinkled and wise. Some are garrulous and love to laugh while some tiptoe and speak almost in whispers. Most are repositories of historical information.

But however divergent their appearance and character, all of them are interesting. Emma Lee, whose career essentially is dealing with dealers, is fiercely loyal to their kind and insists that the hardest task to perform is having to turn a respected dealer down when her show space quota is filled.

That very first Fair was a success on several fronts, but presenting the best of dealers rated right along with Emma Lee's accurate vision of urbanite-moves-to-the-country decorating needs, and instant fame provided by the press. Here are her impressions of some associations that began during the early Round Top shows and grew with the years:

Margaret Richards – Among the Very First

Austin antiques dealers Margaret Richards and Carlo Kilp represented that Texas Capitol city. Many a good collector from Central Texas began their collections with Margaret. She had

the capacity to challenge a collector to upgrade, to reach up to improve their collections. She convinced people to buy the best they could afford. And a whole lot of people followed her lead over many years. Her finds in Austin were often historical ones from a nineteenth century cigar box with former Governor Jim Hogg's portrait on top to discarded nineteenth century legislators chairs from the State Capitol – each with a Texas star emblazoned on the seat.

Margaret has retired from the antiques business but her daughter, Constance Haenggi of Houston, a dealer in toys and other unusual things, carries on the Richards tradition.

Carlo Kilp – Germany to Mexico to Austin to Round Top

Carlo Kilp's background made him an interesting personality on the collecting scene. Carlo immigrated to Austin via Mexico City, when his family fled Germany during World War II.

He brought with him a refined European style which included Oriental rugs and European tapestries and a flair for Bavarian and German pre-Bauhaus furniture and decorative items that reflected his Continental tastes. Carlo was extremely popular with the Texans who were furnishing and decorating their farm houses in areas settled by Germans in the nineteenth century and who found the tie to Germany appealing. Thus, for some, theirs was a re-creation of the more European style with German and Bavarian overtones in their decorating.

Carlo retired to Mexico and lived out his life in a small finca (farmhouse) in a quaint village near Guanajuato. Since it is difficult for antiques dealers to ever really retire, Carlo would return to the states periodically, bringing with him wonderful examples of pre-Colonial Mexican iron hinges and hacienda door locks. Emma Lee remembers one in particular, "This was a lock in the shape of a violin, about eigh-

Highboy dated 1719, to the right a stack of American and Scandinavian painted bride's boxes.
Front of highboy, stuffed lamb pull toy with a working bellows.
On top, a Pennsylvania chalkware lamp, and to the left an American painted bride's box
in the June Worrell Collection. Photo, Betty Tichich

Early 19th century period maple field bed from
the former Ima Hogg Bayou Bend collection with a hand-tied
fish net canopy, June Worrell Collection. Photo, Betty Tichich

teen inches long – these are now highly reproduced. But this was the real thing and as longtime antiques dealer Myrtle Ewell would say 'it was old, old.' These pieces were intricate works of iron art and some of the keys were as much as a foot long. Whenever I'm asked if I regret not buying something along the way, I always think of Carlo's door lock in the shape of a violin."

When Carlo died in early 1990s, it was reported that he left his entire estate to the village which he had enjoyed so much and which had embraced his artistic qualities with warmth and friendship.

June Worrell – Collector First, Dealer Second

Nationally recognized antiques dealer June Worrell was a participant in the early events. Emma Lee describes June as a fun-loving, consummate collector, the bee who finds the sweetest flowers. If offered three highboys, she'll instinctively go for the best one and pay the price. June often gets calls from New England to come decorate Martha's Vineyard estates and houses. Her daughter, Sandra, has been the second generation Worrell showing at Round Top for a number of years as well.

At one show, Emma Lee had a last-minute cancellation so she hurriedly filled in from her own collection which included 600 American coin silver spoons, American Indian baskets and rugs, various small tables and a Texas pie safe which she brought out of her own farm house.

"I had no special attachment to the pie safe," she said, "but June had a small table that interested me. It would be just right for my dining room. So we traded her table for my pie safe.

"The only problem with my end of the arrangement was that June had freshened the finish with a little French polish and it was still tacky. Nevertheless, I thought it would dry in

the back of a pickup truck under the blazing Texas sun. Well, it didn't. I had dinner guests coming that night so I hastily put place mats on the table – and to my chagrin, I had to use the same mats for a year because they permanently stuck to the table.

"June visited me about a year later and I sold the table back to her, place mats and all."

Some years ago when June was invited to do a prestigious show outside of Texas, she asked the show manager if he thought a highboy would be appropriate. "Sure, if you can find one," he replied. "No problem," said June. She had seven.

Laura Ann Rau

Laura Ann of Columbus, Texas, is a descendent of Abraham Alley, one of the original 300 Colonists brought to Texas by Stephen F. Austin. She takes her heritage seriously. As longtime owner of Atascosita Antiques, where she displayed her taste in eighteenth and nineteenth century English porcelain and fine American pieces, she takes great satisfaction in preserving her own area's early houses and decorative arts. Some of her accomplishments:

♦ Raumonda, a large two-story elegant structure with mid-nineteenth century furnishings, in Columbus – she worked with her former husband and still best friend, R. F. "Buddy" Rau.

♦ The Alley family log cabin which had belonged to Laura Ann's aunt, Margaret Griffith, of nearby Alleyton – it was moved to Columbus and furnished with pieces Laura Ann found in the area, antiques she had no intention of selling because she believed they belonged "at home."

Background: Shaker hutch filled with redware and slipware.
Combback and fan back Windsor chairs surround the hutch chair/table.
The 24" American burl bowl on the table is holding a collection
of tin apples that originally came filled with apple candy or were used as
string holders. June Worrell, Houston, Texas. Photo, Betty Tichich

Staffordshire statuary and a platter. Two very popular accessories with Texans. Laura Ann Rau, Atascosita Antiques, Columbus, Texas. Photo, Hickey/Robertson

♦ The Dilue Rose Harris home, furnished in the 1850-period and now a house museum – has a basement, unusual for Texas structures.

♦ The Captain William Hunt House, an 1872 Greek Revival – Captain Hunt fought in the Battle of Bexar, which predated the Alamo confrontation.

♦ The 1863 Gant House moved to Columbus from Alleyton in the early 1980s – has three rooms with the original stenciling and was a recent feature in *Country Living* magazine. Once restored, it was given to the Mary Elizabeth Hopkins Santa Claus Museum.

Buddy Rau is the director of the Visitors and Convention Bureau and he and Laura Ann, who retired as a dealer last year, continue as a dynamic team enviable to communities nationwide. Their efforts are unparalleled in fund raising and reviving the spirit and pride of a small town. They raised $1,300,000 to restore and revitalize the fascinating Columbus Stafford Opera House, calling upon the expertise of Houston architect Barry Moore, FAIA. It is a laurel to rest upon but Buddy recently told Laura Ann about another endangered structure: "You just have to buy this building and save it – it's the oldest commercial building in town." So she did and work on the 1853 relic is in progress. Its destiny? Because there are so many artists in the area, Laura Ann decided, it might become an art gallery.

Eileen Evans

Eileen first appeared at the Round Top show with one of her specialties, cross-stitched Home Sweet Home wall hangings. They were usually in red and white – a compliment to Eileen's very red hair. Over the years, she changed her direction and now specializes in more formal

A Texas-made bed in the booth of Nancy Krause,
Brenham, Texas. Photo, Hickey/Robertson

Vintage saddles with silver ornaments, The Boll Weevil, Calvert, Texas.
Photo, Hickey/Robertson

eighteenth and nineteenth century furniture. With exemplary sources in the East, she always finds something special for Round Top. She and husband Steve have restored two nineteenth Century houses in Chappell Hill, Texas, and live an ideal country life in a charming restored Country Greek revival where they house their Colonial period antiques. In addition to Round Top, their respected collection brings invitations to participate in many of the better Eastern antiques shows.

Nancy B. and Milton Krause

In 1965 the Brenham area was "ripe for the picking," according to Nancy B. Krause, who opened her shop, Nancy's Antiques, that year. Old-timers in the area were happy to sell the furniture they had been living with all their lives.

One woman, who had spent her entire adulthood enduring dark, gloomy pieces hand crafted by early settlers in her German father-in-law's family, made Nancy an offer. She would sell an old dining table for exactly enough money to buy what she had always dreamed about.

Once the deal was done, two women were extremely happy. Nancy was ecstatic because the gloomy table with its Biedermeier-style legs was precisely what the Ladies of Houston were seeking. "It eventually ended up in Faith Bybee's collection," she said. And the seller was thrilled because at last she could go to the local furniture store where she had never been and buy a shiny new chrome dinette set.

Nancy and her husband, Milton, retired public school administrator in Brenham, have spent countless hours restoring early Texas houses. Two of them are decorated in attractive

room settings of Nancy's antiques. Although the Krauses live in Brenham, they have a "play farm" in Chappell Hill, where they've restored a five-room Texas salt box. It's been a great place to socialize with their three children and nine grandchildren. "We do lots of cooking," said Nancy.

She and Milton travel to New England three times a year for a total of eight weeks, in search of antiques to supplement their early Texas finds.

Sallie and Wesley Anderson

Strong community ties keep Sallie and Wesley Anderson in Calvert, Texas, a Victorian gem halfway between Houston and Dallas. Once upon a time it was the fourth largest city in the state, back when cotton was king. Plantation owners built fine Victorian homes in town to represent their prosperity. Then times changed; King Cotton abdicated.

Today Calvert, home to 1,500 with one stoplight, four blocks of antiques and artisan shops, beckons to visitors who crave nostalgia. Thirty-seven complete blocks of Victorian homes are in the National Historic Registry. When Wesley spots a tarnished gem, he likes to buy it, fix it up and rent it until someone with vision buys the home. "I just keep the places pasted together," he said modestly.

"We are not real clubby," said Sallie, explaining that her energy goes into show horses, the shop and, with Wesley, taking fine antiques to a few prestigious shows each year. The Round Top Antiques Fair has been a "must" since it began. Its rush of serious buyers

Canton, Staffordshire and silver, The Boll Weevil, Calvert, Texas.
Photo, Hickey/Robertson

is compelling, but they also look forward to camaraderie with fellow dealers. They still chuckle over June Worrell's antics, one in particular being the year June dashed around in a pair of glasses with one ear piece missing. "Don't laugh – these belonged to Vincent Van Gogh," the irrepressible June was said to declare. A young couple was so amused by the quick comeback, they offered to pay June $20 for the glasses knowing full well that they were participating in a lighter side of the antiques business.

In their booth today, the Andersons might show an extensive collection of Texian Campaign Staffordshire or a Texas table surrounded by horn chairs. There might be fine vintage handmade saddles with silver mounts along with an Audubon or two on the walls.

Sallie Tucker Anderson, whose ancestry goes directly back to the Mayflower, owns "The Boll Weevil" antiques shop. Wesley, a fifth generation Texan, is a cattle rancher. This confident, friendly couple has lived in the same house since their marriage 40 years ago, where they reared four children and now greet three grandchildren.

Mary and Dick Wilmarth –
There's Nothing Older than Moon Rocks

Emma Lee recalls, "When Mary Wilmarth showed with me the first time at one of my Houston Shows at the Shamrock Hilton Hotel, her shop was called 'Mary's Attic.'" She and her husband Dick lived in Clear Lake and Mary was a head of Personnel for NASA while Dick was one of the original scientists and was

among the first to study the moon rocks when they were returned to Earth. "I had always thought it unusual that their interest in antiques was so staunch yet in their professional lives they were involved in outer space and celestial thinking," said Emma Lee. "Then, Barbara Tungate, one of our Show Managers said, 'There is nothing much older than moon rocks,' so I guess it all fits together."

Antiques dealers since 1977, Mary and Dick retired to Brenham for a few years and have now moved to Amarillo to watch every step taken by their grandson. Over the years,

Mary purified her collection and grew in stature as a dealer by always selecting more important and earlier pieces for her customers. For the longest time, she always seemed to find the perfect corner cupboard for Round Top – and it was always blue. Some of her fellow dealers would laugh and say the show wouldn't start until there was a red sold tag on that blue cupboard. It rarely took any time at all. In time, Mary discovered other colors and other types of cabinets and cupboards. She always seemed to have a great early Windsor, a Bride's Box or two, wonderful rugs – just the typical high-style and handsome Wilmarth booth.

◆◆◆◆◆◆◆

A tin toy train from Katie B. Johnson, Westlake, Louisiana.
Antiques Productions collection. Photo, Hickey/Robertson

CHAPTER SEVEN

And Miles and Miles to Go – Gladly

◆◆◆◆◆◆◆◆

Twice a year Betsey Leslie of Running Brook Farm, New Gloucester, Maine, hooks up an antiques-laden fourteen-foot cargo trailer to her Suburban and heads for Round Top, Texas. That's 2,200 miles one way, even more if she detours for shopping.

Making such a trip means she has to hire an animal sitter for her two Angora goats and six sheep and persuade her mother to watch over the dogs, cats, geese and fish. The spinning wheel has to wait, the knitting needles and homegrown yarn are retired temporarily while Betsey has the time of her life.

Sometimes her husband Drew, a landscaper, manages enough time off to accompany her.

"We love to come to Texas," said Betsey. "Everybody at the Round Top Antiques Fair is so enthusiastic. It is my biggest show of the year – I'd come down every month if they'd have me."

The show, however, only happens in spring and fall, and of the two, spring is her favorite traveling time, even though it means missing the Cumberland County Fair. "So my animals don't have any ribbons," she said. "But when we leave Maine, there is snow on the ground. When we get to Texas, they are haying and the

wildflowers are in bloom. The smell of it is wonderful."

Even if Drew is along, Betsey does all the driving. "I don't trust him," she said. "He has a wandering eye – he's forever looking at the passing scenery." But it is Drew who spots antiques shops and Betsey is all too happy to apply the brakes.

The Leslie booth in the Carmine Dance Hall features country painted items and much sought-after Adirondack furniture. The latter, also known as the lodge look, represents great retreats built in the upper New York State mountains by late nineteenth century powerhouses of the American industrial revolution. When collectors relax in a genuine Adirondack chair, they like to imagine the good life enjoyed by those early captains of American industry.

Betsey is relentless in her search for objects at their original source. Consequently, she can present interesting merchandise, often one of a kind, at good prices.

Her dedication, and the fact that she has an excellent reputation in dealing with customers, makes her typical of dealers chosen for the Round Top Antiques Fair, according to Emma Lee, who expects her dealers to be above reproach in serving and pleasing their customers. By her rule, they must bring antiques and collector items of merit that are fresh for the show, not over-shown elsewhere or previously photographed for trade publications.

As Betsey will point out, a good reputation in her business requires muscle power. Lifting those Adirondack chairs and hoisting them into and out of a truck is considerably removed from her gentle hobby of knitting sweaters.

"I do Nautilus every other day to keep in shape, and I do special back exercises," she said.

*A trophy of moose horns hangs above a low-post spindle bed
in Betsey Leslie's booth. Photo, Hickey/Robertson*

Occupying a niche in Marge Maddock's country home is this
New England rope bed with acorn finials, circa 1840.
Its quilt is from the same era, as is the candle box and silhouette
decorating the walls. Photo, Betty Tichich

She also went on a diet a week before Christmas in 1996. "I made dozens of Christmas cookies and didn't even lick my fingers!" She lost fifty-two pounds – all for the sake of the demanding antiques business.

When not in Round Top, she exhibits antiques throughout the East, including Quebec, and is constantly on buying excursions, often a week at a time. She keeps special watch for items with appeal for discriminating Texans. "This business is so all-encompassing," she said. "Fortunately, I have a tolerant husband."

One year her friend Nancy Chesterton, whose specialty is restored trunks, followed her to Round Top and joined the coterie of dealers. "She went through one and one half sales books," said Betsey. "That's about 150 sales!"

After that amazing experience, Nancy understood why Betsey has a love affair with faraway Texas and why she cherishes those invitations to the Round Top Antiques Fair.

◆ ◆ ◆ ◆ ◆ ◆ ◆

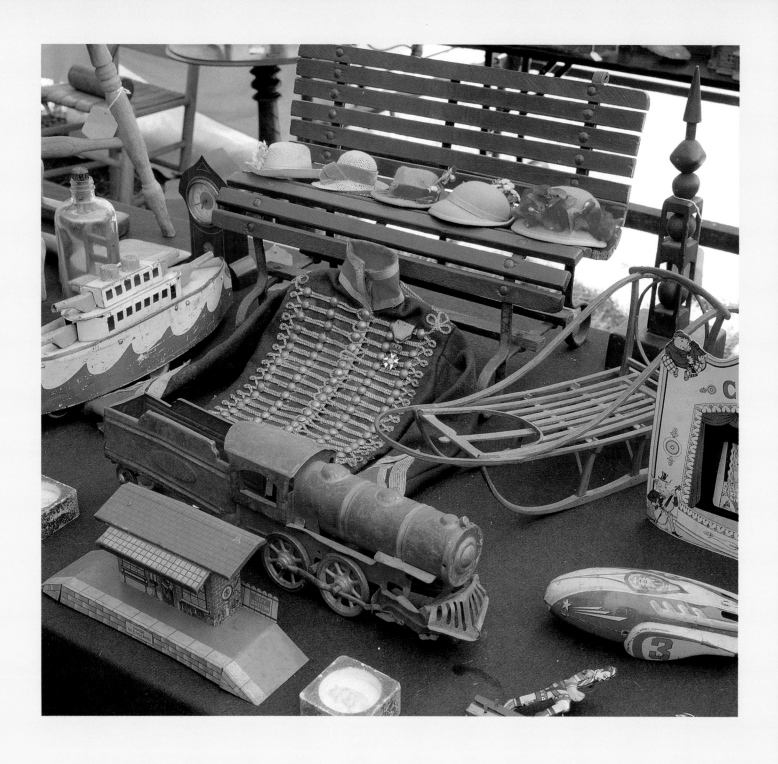

*Emma Lee filled a late minute cancellation with a booth of toys
and salesman's samples. Photo, Hickey/Robertson*

CHAPTER EIGHT

When Antiques Find a Home

♦ ♦ ♦ ♦ ♦ ♦ ♦

LIKE ANY ENDANGERED species, there are limited numbers of antiques in the world. But the hunters, mercifully unarmed unless cash and Argus eyes count, are out in greater numbers.

Marge Maddock

As a newlywed in 1937, Herb Maddock gave his bride $75 to spend for Christmas presents and gifts. She rushed out of the house and came back with an old New England cupboard and a deacon's bench that she didn't intend to give to anyone. That was the beginning of a lifelong hunting season paralleling the chores of rearing children and the manifold duties of volunteer work in Houston.

Thirty years ago she rushed to get in line for Emma Lee's first Round Top show in the Rifle Association Hall. Marge, with her ready smile and eager eyes, was so intrigued by its integrity that she decided absolutely she needed a weekend country home close to the action. She found and updated one of Round Top's originals. Since then, rain or shine, she has patronized the show through the years. Her conquests have included nineteenth century tables, chairs, benches, throws, boxes, baskets and bowls.

An elaborate iron stove from the 19th century dominates the Lawson's kitchen. As a wood burner, it once served a large family in the East. Now it does its work electrically. Photo, Betty Tichich

Marge now lives in retirement down a country lane in a country house filled with country furnishings. She is sitting back and simply enjoying her trophies. They stir a lifetime of pleasant memories – family, friendships, travel, good works, good food around an extended table, good times. But just as enduring are memories of countless antiques trails and the thrills of the hunt.

Janice and French Lawson

If living with antiques is a joy, imagine the pleasure of living within an antique.

City dwellers Janice and French Lawson, longtime patrons of the Round Top Antiques Fair, were lured to country life by their first sight of a place that eventually became a hands-on history lesson. The pre-Republic of Texas two-story double log house, surrounded by ancient live oaks trees, sits on seventy-one acres near Round Top.

Recent visitors drove across a spring-fed creek toward the long porch but Janice waved and motioned to enter the house from the back because a bird was nesting over the front door. With all the woods at hand, the little creature chose to be near humans, and the Lawsons were giving it respect in return.

Original construction on the house, explained Janice and French, was interrupted in 1836 by news that the Mexican General Santa Anna was headed for San Jacinto. Workers

A chair seat that lifts up to reveal storage space for firewood was an organizational necessity of the 19th century. Marge Maddock uses hers with a New England splay-legged one-drawer table. In the background, a four-door cabinet displays an assortment of blue and gray pottery. To the right is a New England chair table draped with a mid-19th century Ohio coverlet. A long-time patron of the show, Marge has used many pieces she found at the Round Top show to furnish her country home. Photo, Betty Tichich

dropped their tools and rode east to do battle for their independence. That accomplished, they finished their carpentry in 1837 for owner Nathaniel Townsend, who had gun ports built over the windows. In those days if it wasn't Santa Anna, it was Indians.

The Lawsons spent four years reconstructing the relic, much of the time spent on research and tracking down artisans who could duplicate methods and materials of the previous century. Janice and French directed the work from temporary accommodations in back of the house. Meanwhile, they built a herd of Texas longhorns that, to the new ranchers' amazement, had all the gentle characteristics of family pets. (Exception: Janice, diving behind a big tree trunk, once learned how protective a mama cow can be of her new offspring. The tense standoff lasted for quite some time.)

In choosing furnishings to complement the historic building's features – original logs, wooden ceilings painted a certain blue, stenciling by Rudolph Melchoir, whose work is also seen at the Winedale Inn – the Lawsons decided that simplicity, even a spare look, was most authentic.

Among antiques to find a home in the Lawson's Texana Plantation were a dozen handmade rawhide chairs and a remarkable iron stove which had once served a large family in the East. The rare tiled and mirrored piece has a warming oven at top, where babies born to the family in bitterly cold months were placed for snug comfort.

Near the fully workable stove (now electric) stands a pioneer Texas pie safe that may be just as remarkable considering its travels. When Maria Lisa, one of the Lawson daughters, attended junior high school in nearby La Grange, she was assigned to bring a sample of genuine Texana or passable replica to class as a history project. The thirteen-year-old was enthusiastic but announced firmly "I don't want to make a plastic Alamo!"

Not surprising in the Lawson family, her solution was to go antique hunting. She paid

$75 for the aged wood and punched tin pie safe. At home she removed its many paint layers to reach natural wood, which she then massaged with paste wax. Hours and hours and days and days of labor later, she persuaded her Dad to hoist it onto his pickup truck and deliver it to school. The cabinet won first place, a well-earned blue ribbon.

When Maria Lisa was ready for college, she reluctantly accepted an offer of $500 for the piece. She needed the money, but it tugged at her heart to let her handiwork go.

Nine years later Janice and French were on a leisurely jaunt to Salado, Texas, when they chanced upon an outdoor antiques show. And there, before their very eyes… could it be? They examined a fine pie safe. Punched into the tin panels were familiar bluebell designs, representing the little wildflower that follows the famous Texas bluebonnet. It had to be Maria Lisa's old history project. They simply couldn't walk away from it. So they bought it.

French positioned it on the front porch where their daughter would have to spot it when she came home for a visit. Sure enough, with a squeal Maria Lisa recognized her blue ribbon winner. It had come home again – this time for $1200!

◆ ◆ ◆ ◆ ◆ ◆ ◆

This yellow racer came from Carol and George Meekins,
Preston, Maryland. Antiques Productions collection.
Photo, Hickey/Robertson

CHAPTER NINE

Great Show – Great Words!

◆◆◆◆◆◆◆

ROUND TOP, TEXAS, has an extraordinary scrapbook of press clippings accumulated over many years. The focus of much of it is Emma Lee Turney's internationally famous Round Top Antiques Fair, which had its beginning before there were bed and breakfast inns, before the artists from outside settled in.

Typically, her constant effort toward publicizing and advertising her show in the national home design magazines and other publications has been useful to other activities in the area.

If anything, the publicity escalates. The scrapbook increased in size recently when

Country Living, Country Home, Getaways, Southern Accents and *Texas Highways* magazines produced major features. Also, Charles Osgood of CBS News Sunday Morning sent producer Mary Mapes and correspondent Bob McNamara from the CBS Dallas division to produce a feature on the Round Top Antiques Fair. Photographer Hank Bargine from Colorado and soundman Eric Williams from New Mexico were part of the team.

In the early nineties, the ABC Home Show sent designer Kitty Bartholomew to the show that was featured in a design and collecting segment on the show.

More recently the *Houston Chronicle*, to supplement regular seasonal reports, sent reporter Clifford Pugh to the mini-town ninety miles away for an overview of its cultural and fine arts activities. His story was played on page one, a logical position given that Round Top had been listed in John Villani's book, *The 100 Best Small Art Towns in America*. Villani had been assigned by *Southern Accents* to cover Emma Lee's Antiques Fair. He came away truly impressed with her show and the town's overall sensitivity to art and restoration.

Here's What Some of the Best Have Had to Say

"Stop, Even Shop at Round Top" and "Houstonians Lead Way in Restoration of Tiny Town" read the headlines in the first four-color front page Women's Section of the *Houston Chronicle*, dated March 30, 1969. This feature appeared the Sunday before the second show and reinforced the already fascinating interest in the area by people across the State of Texas. Throughout the 1970s, there was substantial follow-up with continuing news stories about the progress in restoration being made at Round Top and the presentation of the twice a year Antiques Fair. The dealers were selling and the buyers were buying.

In 1982, San Antonio collectors and writers Virginia and Clark Munroe, who had been avid patrons of the show since its early beginnings, wrote a review of the show for *Maine Antique Digest*, published in Waldoboro, Maine. It has become known as the "Woman Hollaring" article because it caused an avalanche of calls from New England dealers eager to participate in the show in order to reach such a good market of collectors. It also caused a rush of new patrons

from distant states. Here's how it began:

"You go East and cross over Woman Hollaring Creek, turn North on the road that used to take you to the 'Chicken Ranch,' (the best little whorehouse in Texas, made famous by the Broadway play of the same name), and then swoosh down the winding country road past fields wild with bluebonnets, Indian paintbrush and buttercups." This was Virginia and Clark's introduction of Round Top to the Eastern Establishment of collectors and dealers.

To further quote the Munroes, "If you have never 'made' Round Top, you have missed something. It is a first-rate country antique show with a reputation for having had more outstanding Texana sold through the years than in any other show in the state. It has good dealers, good customers, and good food. At one table, there were four generations from the same family enjoying the German food with homemade kolaches that melt in your mouth. Inside the exhibit area, the 'regulars' milled knowledgeably among the booths while newcomers quickly realized what the others knew - this was a show unique in Texas.

"Outside, pickups vied with Mercedes for parking spaces under the oaks. The scraps of conversation mirrored the clientele. 'This is the best Round Top in years.' 'We just took our group to Williamsburg. Did you see Mary Emmerling? She's doing a home feature for *House Beautiful...*'

'It is a place where friends know they will meet without prearrangement, because missing Round Top is like missing a family reunion.'"

Emma Lee said, "Virginia recently wrote to me that during one Antiques Fair an

unheard of activity had been planned that would interfere with her joining us. A relative was getting married. Virginia's husband, Clark, offered to have her flown to the show by helicopter but happily she was able to make the show anyway."

Patrons and dealers throughout the history of the show have expressed this kind of loyalty. There have even been times when long-time patrons have writ-ten notes saying why they couldn't attend!

As the show grew in both numbers of exhibitors and in attendance, it became appealing to feature writers from across the state. Word spread and editors of major national publications such as *Country Living* took notice and sent writers to feature the show and write "House" and design articles.

◆ ◆ ◆ ◆ ◆ ◆ ◆

Carol and George Meekins, Preston, Maryland,
on Sunday morning. Photo, Hickey/Robertson

The Fayette County Record

La Grange, TX, September 30, 1983

"Round Top Antiques Fair Features New York Author"

"Mary Ellisor Emmerling could have selected to drive less than a hundred miles from her Manhattan loft to stage a major autographing session of her new book "Collecting American Country" in the heart of the source of antiques in New England, New York and Pennsylvania. Up there, antiques shows often present as many as 1000 exhibitors and attract crowds of 20,000. Instead Mary is coming to tiny Round Top to introduce her beautiful book at the Round Top Antiques Fair.

"…Round Top Antiques Fairs are well known in the East, Mary included sections on The Winedale Historical Center and Henkel Square in her first book."

Santas in all shapes and sizes shown in a holiday booth.
Photo, Hickey/Robertson

Hixson, Tennessee's Shane Campbell brought this huge butcher shop sign in the shape of a pig. Photo, Hickey/Robertson

Gossip Columnist, Marge Crumbaker

The Houston Post

October 3, 1985

"ZUM ZUM GANG – Antiques biggie Emma Lee Turney will toss an autographing party for best-selling author Mary Emmerling on Saturday during the Antiques Fair at Round Top. Mary, a former editor at *House Beautiful* and *Mademoiselle,* will be signing the first copies of *American Country West,* her style and source book.

"Everyone who is rediscovering the western pride in hand carved crafts, down-home rusticity and cowboy charisma, will want this book. Mary is a master at collecting and putting things together and sharing those ideas with her readers. Her popular *American Country* and *Collecting American Country* books

helped us bring the western spirit into our homes.

"Just for the records, she's the great-granddaughter of William Henry Harrison, the ninth president of the United States. Harrison was the son of a signer of the Declaration of Independence, so you can see that Mary has wonderful credentials."

In 1986, popular *Country Living* Editor-at-Large, Niña Williams featured the Antiques Fair in a centerspread highlighting the beauty of the show. *Country Living* featured Texas country houses as well, in honor of the Texas Sesquicentennial. Niña's comment about the show was "…it's simply irresistible."

A look at Woody Straub's booth, Antiques and the Arts,
Panacea, Florida. Photo, Hickey/Robertson

Marge Crumbaker

The Houston Post

September 27, 1987

"RICH AND FAMOUS – The Round Top Antiques Fair is on tap Saturday and Sunday. It is the BIG ONE as far as the local carriage trade is concerned. Almost all of the area's farm and ranch owners turn out in force."

Any booth by O'Neill-Leonard, Austin, Texas
is stunning. Photo, Hickey/Robertson

The Houston Post

April 8, 1988

"…annual Round Top Antiques Fair …features Madalene Hill autographing her new book, *Southern Herb Growing. Maine Antique Digest* writer Virginia Munroe will be saluted with the Round Top Award in Journalism signed by Governor Wm. P. Clements and Awards founder Emma Lee Turney."

California dealer, Mary Millman shows an assortment of country furniture, textiles and doll houses. Photo, Hickey/Robertson

Antiques West

San Francisco, CA, December, 1989

"There is simply no other show like it in Texas. There's an indescribable quality to Round Top, a kind of aura that doesn't occur at many other shows anywhere. Some people even save their money so they can say with a bit of pride, 'Oh yes, I found that at Round Top.' It's exciting to collectors and participating dealers alike."

Santos and Christos in Patti Howell's booth, Austin, Texas. Photo, Hickey/Robertson

Moving into the 1990s

One of the big attractions at the Antiques Annex and Folk Art Fair is the display window filled with articles about the Antiques Fair. Patrons and dealers alike always want to see the latest articles written about the show.

Selecting articles and headlines is about as difficult as selecting dealers. So many good ones, which ones to include?

Emma Lee said, "Each article is so special to us and serves as a reminder of not only the star quality of the dealers in the show, but the good times we always have when visiting writers, editors and news media attend.

"The 1990s brought us more of the same in Texas but we were also honored by a visit from *Country Living* Editor-in-Chief Rachel Newman, Niña Williams, Editor-at-Large of *Country Living Gardener,* and Special Events Editor, Marylou Krajci. These three top editors for the Hearst Corporation had been in the Caribbean on a business trip and went through a lot of difficulty to get to us. They flew from the Bahamas to Atlanta, changed planes to fly to Houston's Hobby Airport on the Southeast side of town, rented a car and drove the approximately ninety miles to Round Top. They spent all day getting to us. Rachel Newman has been generous in her coverage of both the show and in giving a peek into the living rooms, kitchens and lifestyles of Texan's country houses." During this trip they autographed their very popular book, *Living with Folk Art.* Marylou Krajci often represents the magazine at the autographing of their latest books.

After that memorable visit Marylou Krajci returned with photographer Keith Scott Morton and they produced a two-page spread on the Antiques Fair and articles on Frances and Bill Harris' Heart of My Heart Ranch Bed and Breakfast and Karen and Larry Beevers' The Settlement House at Round Top.

Texas antiques dealer Patti Walsh, who was a feature in the article on the Antiques Fair, was amazed to receive calls and letters from people in Alaska, California, Arizona and Australia.

Country Living Special Projects Editor, Marylou Krajci, is a popular visitor at Round Top. Shown here autographing the book Country Look. *Texans still talk about a recent visit by Editor-in-Chief, Rachel Newman,* Country Living *Gardner Editor-at-Large, Niña Williams and Marylou Krajci who came to the Antiques Fair to present their book,* Living with Folk Art. *They left from a Hearst Corporation meeting in the Caribbean, flew to Atlanta, Georgia, changed planes, flew on to Houston's Hobby Airport, rented a car, drove to Round Top (approximately ninety miles from that area), arriving at Round Top well into the night. Their books were sold out next day in a few short hours. Photo, Madeleine McDermott Hamm*

Madeleine McDermott Hamm
Home Design Editor
Houston Chronicle
March 31, 1989

"ANTIQUES FAIR BLOSSOMS AMONG WILDFLOWERS."

"To a Texan, the first weekend in April means bluebonnets. To an antiques-loving Texan, the first weekend in April means driving to the Round Top Antiques Fair and enjoying bluebonnets and other wildflowers along the way.

"The Round Top Antiques Fair is one of those extraordinary traditions like the Livestock Show and Rodeo parade in downtown Houston or the First Baptist Church Christmas pageant – that you must see to appreciate."

above: Green jelly cupboard. Photo, Hickey/Robertson

above right: Antiquarian children's books in Barbara Meyer's booth, Georgetown, Texas. Photo, Hickey/Robertson

Madeleine McDermott Hamm

Houston Chronicle

April 14, 1990

COUNTRY WITH CLASS

A review of the show pointed out that maybe country really isn't a good label for the show any longer, not if you thought of country as bales of hay and just rockers on the front porch. This article pointed out the thousands of collectors who show up in Cadillacs and Jeep Cherokees. And the women in designer denims and diamonds buying everything in sight from advertising tins to coverlets and quilts "…and collectors buy quickly, for after all if they don't, there are others in line to take their place."

Mariana Greene

Dallas Morning News

May 26, 1991

"…Round 'um up for Round Top and head to the best antique show in Texas…some say the best West of the Mississippi, others say the best in the country…"

Mariana Greene, a former feature writer for the Dallas Morning News, had long been a fan of the Antiques Fair ever since she was the Editor-in-Chief of the monthly magazine Texas Homes. During her career with Texas Homes, she was one of the editors responsible for the statewide focus on interior design and gardens. Styling their surroundings to appeal to the staff at Texas Homes so their house or garden might be featured became a new sport among readers.

"When the owners of Texas Homes stopped publishing, it was on assignment for the Dallas Morning News that Mariana came to Round Top and conducted interviews among dealers and patrons alike that resulted in one of our most treasured headlines," said Emma Lee.

A huge blue and gray cupboard and a good New England candle stand.
Photo, Hickey/Robertson

Gayle Green's collection of iron door stops. Photo, Hickey/Robertson

Houston Chronicle

April 3, 1992

"ALL ROADS LEAD TO TINY ROUND TOP...because this is a major event for country collectors, most dealers buy especially for this show and hold back important pieces for the Round Top crowd."

This statement was mirrored by the comments from Jackson, Mississippi, antiques dealers, John and Carolyn Heiden when they wrote: "We had the largest show in sales we've ever had. We feel like your suggestion to dealers to search for the 'special pieces' and save them for Round Top is paying off for us..."

Madeleine McDermott Hamm

Houston Chronicle

September 27, 1992

Featured on the front cover of the Sunday supplement, *Texas Magazine*

"For 25 years, the Antiques Fair in tiny Round Top has been THE BEST SHOW IN TOWN...Turney's event...'Put Round Top on the map,' as the saying goes."

Grace Homan, Austin, Texas, presents a booth with pewter and a large country table filled with fruit. Photo, Hickey/Robertson

Folk pieces in twig, wire, beadwork, basketry and tramp art. Photo, Hickey/Robertson

Gay Elliott McFarland
Style
The Houston Post
October 2, 1993

"THE LURE OF ROUND TOP"
"Top drawer interior designers, politicos, TV anchors and collectors from as far away as Saudia Arabia make a point to attend Oktoberfest Round Top Antiques Fair...and the faithful attendees know that the dealers travel throughout the country to find wonderful antiques for this show...no matter what the weather, trust me, people have waded in ankle-deep mud to attend...and the show goes on."

Kitty Bartholomew

ABC Home Show Design Feature

October 1993

"…the Buys of Texas, it's impossible to leave empty handed…" from a ten minute segment from Los Angeles.

Left to right: Leah Smirlis, Art Director, and Editor Mimi Handler of Early American Life (now Early American Homes) came to the Round Top Antiques Fair to present their 25th anniversary edition. Features in the magazine included Steve and Eileen Evans' Greek Revival restoration and Elizabeth and the late Houston architect Harvin C. Moore's Stagecoach Inn at nearby Chappell Hill, Texas; the National Wildflower Research Center founded by Lady Bird Johnson; the article Frontier Classic, Plans for A Dog-Run House by Barry Moore, FAIA, and the Round Top Antiques Fair. Photo, Karla Klein Albertson

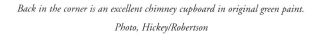

Back in the corner is an excellent chimney cupboard in original green paint. Photo, Hickey/Robertson

Deborah Mann Lake
Design Line Editor
The Houston Post
April 10, 1994

"The show is considered one of the best in the United States for country antiques…"

Madeleine McDermott Hamm

Home Design Editor

Houston Chronicle

October 30, 1994

OUTSIDERS INSIDERS

"A garden is a wonderful place to tuck away a tiny bench to sit among the plantings for a few moments of private meditation."

This review of the Oktoberfest show highlighted the architectural and garden ornaments that appeared in profusion. Pointing out that for many new gardeners there is more to it than planting seeds. The use of well placed urns, fancy iron birdbaths and tables of mosaic and iron have their place right along with the beds of vegetables and flowers

This collecting segment is enjoying a second renaissance from the late 1950s to the early 1970s. Twenty-five to thirty years ago, many of the Victorian buildings and houses in such towns as St. Louis, Chicago and dozens of other mid-west cities were being dismantled to make way for urban renewal. The architectural elements from the fine old structures were just as highly sought after then as they are today.

During the 1950s and 1960s, the advent of the patio as an addition to practically every new house being built increased the demand for garden furniture.

above: Few examples of this original concrete garden art remain. This set is from San Antonio and was constructed around the 1920s by two artisans from the same family. Both had worked on the palace in Mexico City where they learned the art form. The artisans used twigs and paint brushes to sculpt the pieces and each piece was painted to resemble a tree. They were so secretive about the process that the art form is almost extinct. There are a few examples that remain in San Antonio parks. Ann Gunnells Collection, Seabrook, Texas. Photo, Cynthia Anderson

left: One of the famous Grenfell hooked rugs shown by Douglas Fairlee, Austin, Texas. These mats and rugs have become most popular and are sought after by collectors since a show sponsored by the Museum of American Folk Art in New York City. That show was reviewed by Marjorie Chesterman for Maine Antique Digest *and appeared in the July, 1994 issue. Photo, Karla Klein Albertson*

Mrs. George W. (Laura) Bush, First Lady and wife of the Governor of Texas on a Round Top visit with her friend, Dallas, Texas, garden and architectural dealer, Betty Sewell. Photo, Karla Klein Albertson

The Country Gentleman, Larry Bahn, Houston, Texas on red, white and blue day. Photo, Hickey/Robertson

Judy P. Sopronyi
Managing Editor
Early American Life
(now *Early American Home*)
Harrisburg, PA, April 1994

"Say Round Top to anyone interested in antiques and chances are they'll think of the Round Top Antiques Fair."

Karla Klein Albertson
Antique Review
Worthington, OH
May 1994

"What's so special about the Texas Market?"

Larry N. Bahn, The Country Gentleman, Houston, Texas: "The marvelous thing that I see happening now is a lot of people from the East and West Coasts are seeing that this is a buyers' market, and they're now coming. I had shoppers from California; there's supposedly a lady from New York here buying for five shops…I mean, nothing against my Eastern friends, but it's a hot market!"

Antique Print and Map Dealer, Barbara Tungate: "…what we have here in Texas are people who are very knowledgeable, very particular in their tastes. They don't like things that are highly refinished, they want the original surfaces. They are connoisseurs."

Cathy and Mike Harmon, Campbell, Texas, garden and architectural ornaments. Photo, Hickey/Robertson

John Villani
Southern Accents
Birmingham, AL
March–April 1994

"ANTIQUING TEXAS STYLE   Attracting visitors from coast to coast, the Round Top Antiques Fair is one of the country's premier antiques events."

Jamie Mercier and Richard Beecher

The Antiques Journal

Ware, MA

November 1995

"The word was out that Round Top was first rate, and Emma Lee modestly attributes its unqualified success to the 'ability of major antiques dealers to sustain quality year after year.'

"It's not a secret that dealers truly love this show. Every year they buy special, fresh merchandise in anticipation of their trip to Round Top, and show-goers are never disappointed. Great stuff, and I do mean great, is at Round Top."

Brenham, Texas, dealer Margaret Shanks' garden booth. Photo, Hickey/Robertson

Country Home

Des Moines, IA

July/August 1996

Former Houston writer, Gary McKay, Interior Design Editor for *Country Home,* returned to Texas and was joined by writers Joetta Moulden, Larry Erickson and photographer William Stites in several features which included Briarfield Bed and Breakfast, Festival Institute, Virginia and Robin Elverson's Walnut Hill Farm, Beverly and Tommy Jacomini's 5J Farm, Gaste Haus Round Top and Outpost at Cedar Creek B & B.

Feature writer Karla Klein Albertson included a story on the Antiques Fair saying that "Show weekends crackle with the energy of collecting."

Olive Weimert, Missouri City, Texas, can be counted on to bring some very famous and very special teddy bears. Photo, Hickey/Robertson

David Drummond, Lititz, Pennsylvania. Photo, Hickey/Robertson

Karla Klein Albertson

Quilts Magazine

Des Moines, IA

Fall 1996

"Antique quilts flourish at the original Rifle Hall site and within the huge Great White Tent nearby. The softly-filtered light under the white canvas makes every careful stitch and colorful scrap stand out as thousands of visitors walk the aisles."

Carol Barrington

Texas Highways

March 1997

"And why do thousands of antique-hunters return to Round Top year after year?

"Antique quilt exhibitor Terry Browder of Abilene zeros in on the reason for the show's success: 'It's the quality of the dealers,' he says. 'Their knowledge and buying abilities bring the very best of American country antiques to Round Top. The quality is there, and the prices are good. I buy at shows from other dealers – that's one of the ways I conduct business – and I buy big at Round Top. Emma Lee Turney doesn't let junk in her show, and she doesn't compromise quality. As a result, buyers know they can find good antiques at reasonable prices.'"

Ann Sams: "For dealers it is very prestigious to show at Round Top – it's not just any show. As many other dealers do, I always buy special things just to sell at this show. And, why buy new when a beautiful handmade piece that's 100 years old goes for the same price?"

A green cupboard and two colorful green, white and red quilts.
Photo, Hickey/Robertson

Karla Klein Albertson

Antiques and the Arts Weekly

Newtown, CT,

June 20, 1997

"Buyers arrive in droves - from the Northeast, Chicago or California – firmly convinced that they have found a great source for antiques with the right look…dealers displays range from traditional New England settings to eclectic fantasies, but, within this variance, a distinctive Round Top style has developed."

American Indian corn husk bags, Joan Wilson, Chandler, Texas.
Photo, Hickey/Robertson

A collection of Skookam dolls. Photo, Hickey/Robertson

119

A warm country setting in a room with stenciled walls. Photo, Hickey/Robertson

Those are Alaskan Mukluks (boots) on the shelf in Austin, Texas, dealer Grace Homan's booth. Photo, Hickey/Robertson

David Anderson

Maine Antique Digest

Waldoboro, ME

June 1997

"In the Rifle Hall, we found ample choices of quality eighteenth and early nineteenth century American furniture, quilts and linens, flat art, and silver. Windsor chairs, tables, cupboards, beds, desks, and secretaries abounded. Most of these were competitively priced, and there were a number of choice high-dollars items displayed. Most dealers reported 'excellent' sales."

A splendid example of a copper finial. Ann Gunnells, Seabrook, Texas.

Photo, Betty Tichich

Charles Osgood's

CBS News Sunday Morning

New York, NY

April 1997

"When the (Antique) Fair opens, it looks like opening night. She's (founder Emma Lee Turney) watched the country look gain Madison Avenue cache…for her, the reward is in seeing new appreciation for small town treasures…It isn't the scenery that draws crowds to tiny Round Top…it is the Round Top Antiques Fair…it's the best…Round Top has become a decorating Mecca…"

Bob McNamara, Commentator

Texas horn chair, Susan Franks, Austin, Texas.
Photo, Hickey/Robertson

CHAPTER TEN

Emma Lee's Views on Country Courtesies

♦♦♦♦♦♦♦

THERE IS NO SUCH THING as an abandoned farmhouse. Yet, for reasons I don't understand, some visitors to the country forget their manners and courtesies. They seem to think it is perfectly all right to enter property uninvited and peer into windows.

During the early 1970s, all but one of my Texas houses was in various stages of restoration. I used the one as my headquarters and retreat as often as I could. It was furnished with Texas furniture that had been made in the Round Top area – much of which my neighbors Erna and Wilbur Marburger had traded to

me for the worn tin on the roofs of the houses. I had replaced the tin roofs with cedar wood shingles.

You can imagine my shock when one day I received a call from a Houston area attorney who asked if I wanted to sell my farmhouse. He described how much he liked what he had seen as he was "poking around." When I asked if he took a fancy to my Houston home, would he walk up to the windows and "poke around," he was insulted and said "Certainly not!" When I went on to ask why he had chosen to trespass on my property when it was evident I wasn't there, he had no answer. You can guess the tone of my voice when I went on about never climbing fences and gates – and the reason why we have fences and gates in the country. A real good reason is to keep folks like him out.

So, one of the first rules about visiting in the country: Never, ever, go on someone's property without first being invited.

Rules of courtesy in the country are often more strict than in the city. I talked with friends who grew up in the country and asked for a bit of input. As a former Texan raised on a ranch, Connie Going had quite a bit to say, as did a few others. Some country sayings are also included which might lead to better understanding.

♦ Just because a property doesn't have a "Posted" sign doesn't mean you're free to go on it. Sometimes, such signs are not put up purposely to insure that the Volunteer Fire Department will know it's okay to enter to put out a fire.

♦ Never enter a gate if someone is not expecting you.

♦ Never leave a gate open.

♦ If it is absolutely necessary for you to call on someone uninvited, lightly hit your horn to announce your presence and call out "hello" before ever setting foot on the porch. Usually a knock is unnecessary. But a "hello" is very important.

♦ Do drive very slowly when passing or approaching riders on horses and across pastures of cows. DON'T honk the car horn or yell.

♦ Do give a friendly little wave back at oncoming traffic.

♦ If you see a funeral procession approaching, pull off to the side of the road to show respect until the entire procession has passed.

♦ Don't go on someone's fenced property to pick pine cones, berries, take pictures in the bluebonnets or to try to pet the cute Brahma bull.

The punched tin door panels and strong pediment
make this an unusual wardrobe. Photo, Hickey/Robertson

Wind-up tin fireman still climbs his ladder.
Antiques Productions Collection. Photo, Hickey/Robertson

- Don't assume the guy on the tractor is a hick. Chances are, along with his work ethic, he also has a college degree and active oil wells on the north 40.

If all goes well and you're invited to visit, here are a few items that might prove useful:

- Don't ask how much land they own or how many heads of cattle they're running. That's the same thing as asking how much money they have in the bank.
- Don't wear one pant leg in your boot.
- Don't wear chaps or spurs, unless you're going on a round-up.

Translations:

- Don't think when they say 'Come back now, you hear?' they mean right this instant. It's simply a way to end an encounter.
- "Born days," means whole life or 'all my life' – 'I've never seen such a thing in all my born days.'
- "I don't care if I do," means "I accept."
- "Oh, get out!" means "I don't believe you" when told the bucket is from the 1700s.
- "You gotta own up," means to admit the truth.
- Breakfast is breakfast but lunch is dinner and dinner is supper.
- "Evening " is the shank of the afternoon.
- "Fix your own plate," doesn't mean get out the glue. It means serve yourself.

In other words, just act pretty much as you would in town – with respect for the surroundings, the people and the property – and you will always be welcome.

Emma Lee Turney

Doris Cantrell, New Ulm, Texas, Texas table and sofa.
Photo, Hickey/Robertson

CHAPTER ELEVEN

Emma Lee Thanks Her Friends

◆ ◆ ◆ ◆ ◆ ◆ ◆

HOW BIG can a thank you be? When I think of what has made this show a success, I think of the excellent dealers who work so hard, travel so far and make such an outstanding effort to present the best antiques they can find. I think of the patrons of this show some of whom have missed very few during our thirty years. I think of the new collectors who are traveling from both coasts to be with us. I think of how can I make this easier for everyone. Also, I think of my unsung heroes and friends who work behind the scenes to make this weekend run smoothly and to be sure it is a safe, secure and successful show.

Without These People, There Would Be No Round Top

Top of the list of heroes has to be Betty Burch Meyer, my wonderful friend who has worked with me for thirty-six years. Betty is always there for us with a big smile and great costuming. She's the one who shows up as an elf at Christmas time, a Leprechaun on St. Patrick's Day and even has glow-in-the-dark eyeball earrings for Halloween. We can't wait to see what she'll wear to the next Round Top. She is in charge of admissions, office management, compiling hundreds of dealer information packets and seeing to it that all of our office equipment is moved to Round Top from Houston for the administration of the show. She is a shoulder to lean on when clouds are dark and in her quiet way sees that everything we need to run the show is right where it is supposed to be. My thanks also to Thom and Lil Vickers, Mary Shannon, Alison Nelson and Gary Burris who work with Betty on admissions.

Nelson and Ann Aschenbeck are the ringmasters at the Great White Tent where Nelson is in charge of exhibitor set-up. I can't count the different duties they perform during this weekend. Nelson and Nathan Kalkhake work all year on the grounds and in maintaining the properties. They are the ones who always have something in a toolbox that can repair anything and a tractor to pull vehicles out of the mud during times of inclement weather. Ann is in charge of seeing that all supplies are on hand for keeping grounds and buildings tidy and is Nelson's right hand during unloading. Earl Neumann, Brady Gregor, Jason Wagner, Clark Krueger, Brandon Krwaika, Brad Hinze, Blake Goehring and Clay Goehring join them working at the Great White Tent.

Ken Thuesen and Harold M. Smith take great care of the Rifle Hall dealers and have been joined in the past by Kevin Smith and Daniel Orsak.

Dan Kienstra comes to Round Top from Galveston, Texas, to set up the Antiques Annex and Folk Art Fair and as dealer Alan Hoops from Findlay, Ohio, said to me during one show, "You just don't have any idea how much help Dan is to the dealers and how much he is doing for the show." Well, I do know that Dan never stops until all jobs are finished, from seeing that the dealers are set-up on Thursday and are safely on their way home Sunday afternoon. Making sure that the grounds are kept maintained during the show and directing the parking directors and keeping the flow of traffic running smoothly both into the show and on the grounds all falls into his area of responsibility. Joining Dan at the Antiques Annex and Folk Art Fair location are Glenn Krause and Michael Reznicek, who always comes to my rescue with a few more fine men of the community to help as parking directors. These

include Guy McKee, Michael Nobloch, Joshua Limmer, Judson Limmer Joah Weidemann, Jordan Weidemann, and Ryan Hinze who divides his time between Round Top and Carmine.

At the Carmine Dance Hall I want to thank my very dear friends Berrie Etzel, Glenn Treude and Elvis Hinze who see that the exhibitors are unloaded and set-up with such ease and then go on to other duties such as service with the barbecue staff during the weekend. They are joined by Floyd Etzel, Clint Etzel, Kevin Hinze, Jeff Flinn, Jarrett Stork and Robbie Stork. The preparation for the barbecue lunches are handled by Ralph and Elsa Marth, Donald Watkins, Milton Fisher, Tony Dooley, Walter Schautschick, Sylvia Sanders, Jocie Jacob, Jeff Flinn, Cindy Hinze, Leroy and Ora Lee Levien, Darlene Etzel, Cheryl Etzel,

Howard and Joyce Fuchs and Stuart and Susie Markwardt.

With Great appreciation I want to thank the members and their wives for the continued good job they do in preparing barbecue lunches at the Rifle hall. Those members are: President Ronnie Siptak, Jim Ayres, Erwin V. Bayer, Gerald L. Beaver, Harold Bergmann, Marvin Dallmeyer, Fritz Finke, Edgar Fricke, Jr., Jeff Fricke, Edwin Gau, Jr., Jeff Gau, Barney Lee Georges, William M. (Bill) Harris, Clarence Hinze, Delphine Hinze, Eldor Hinze, Otto Hinze, Jr. David Jaster, Douglas J. Knutzen, Dan Kolenovsky, Calvin Paul Krause, Glenn Krause, Weldon G. Krause, Eugene Menke, Lee Dell Neutzler, Bruce Noak, Nolan Noak, Dwayne Oltmann, Kirby Gene Oltmann, Fred H. Oppermann, Ronnie Sacks, Willie Sacks, Jr., Donald E. Schlaudraf, Arthur Siptak, *right: Bill Bowles, euphonium; Band Leader, Ronny Sacks, tenor horn; Joe Lewis, tuba; Michael Reznicek, drums; Betty Sacks, accordion. Ronny Sacks can quickly change his hat to become Fire Chief of the Volunteer Round Top Fire Department or President and CEO of the Round Top State Bank or chicken and sausage server in the barbecue line. Along with husband Ronny, Betty Sacks is owner and proprietor of the Round Top Mercantile. When son Michael Reznicek comes home from college during the Antiques Fair he serves as parking director for the Antique Annex and Folk Art Fair. Photo, Bernice Umlan*

Ron R. Stork, Vastine Treybig, Edward C (Archie) Veith, Edrol Wagner, Oliver (Dick) Wagner, Robert Wagner, Steven Wagner, Wayne Wagner and Donald Watkins, Edward F. Wegner, Dave Weishuhn, Herman Weigelt, Ridge Wessels, Milton Wickel and Wayne Wolle.

The Rifle Hall Membership Auxiliary ladies who serve for their organization in the various duties in connection with the dining room: Delores Bayer, Barbara Baranoski, Wendy Beaver, Margaret Charlesworth, Katie Cordes, Betty Dallmeyer, Esse Lee Fricke, Aleine Finke, Cathy Gau, Frances Gau, Inez Gebhard, Dorothy Giese, Nola Goehring, Grace Hinze, Ira Mae Hinze, Rosa Lee Hinze, Frances Harris, Amy Wagner Hooge, LaVerna Jacobs, Loraine Kneip, Cecil Krause, Gladys Krause, Esther Krause, Martha Leonhardt, Michele Marburger, Rose Marburger, Peggy Marburger, Jennifer Marburger, Ruth Menke,

Mae Neidig, Vernell Noak, Shirley Neumann, Nadine Neutzler, Mary Jane Oltmann, Eunice Quade, Arline Schlaudraff, Betty Sacks, Ora Nell Sacks, Laurie Story, Ida Schmidt, Leander Schlabach, Garda Siptak, Trina Siptak, Caroline Trusty, Elfrieda Treude, Bernice Reed, Martha Veith, Lesia Wagner, Virginia Wagner, Perlie Wagner, Marilyn Wagner, Rebecca Wagner, Barbara Wagner, Lanette Williams, Lisa Weishuhn, Tina Wagner, Verlie Wegner, Sharon Wunderlich and Angelina Zwernemann.

Thanks also to Clarence Wagner, Kermit and Nelda Wunderlich, Roger and Sharon Wunderlich, Doris Georges, Sheriff Rick Vandel and Constable Milton Zinglemann, Lee Richards, Butch and Linda Karstedt, Milton and Elaura Neumann, Harvey Lee Albers and Roland Nester. Roland Nester bought my beloved Briarfield home and comes to my rescue to help with book signings, exhibitor set-ups, looking after our needs for everything from seeing that my flower beds are planted to hosting an impromptu buffet when we're over-run with special guests. He's a true friend in deed, whenever I have the need.

My very special thanks to Annie and Robert F. Banik for allowing us to lease the adjoining six acres next to the Rifle Hall for additional parking. The Banik's spirit of community concern brought them to us just as we found we needed more safe, off-road parking. It is people like the Baniks and others in the community including the Do Your Duty service club who help make the weekend an enjoyable experience.

Karen and Bud Royer and children, Tara, Micah, Todd and J.B. who work in Royer's Round Top Café with them, are one of the most talented and dedicated families to move to the Round Top area in recent years. Their restaurant was selected by Zagat's national restaurant survey as the best country restaurant in the Houston guide, even though Houston is

90 miles away. My thanks to Karen and Bud for making our weekend so special and showing such respect for our exhibitors and patrons who travel from coast to coast. Bud always makes room for one more table for our guests from national home design publications and the news media that join us for the weekend.

Although I was flattered that Madeleine McDermott Hamm has said that I "put Round Top on the map" with the Antiques Fair, I will have to share that distinction with my friend Bud Royer. Bud has participated in food shows from New York to California presenting his delicious pies, Sinammon rolls and pepper sauces. He is never at a loss in thinking up new recipes for the restaurant or in spreading the word about the café and Round Top. It was a true blessing for the town the day the Royers moved to Round Top.

My longtime friends, Liz and Ronald Klump operate Klump's Café that offers a taste of real home-style cooking. Theirs is the place for fried catfish on Friday nights, barbecue on

Saturday and fried chicken dinners on Sunday. Liz and Ronny are local (meaning descendants of original settlers) and are to be complimented on staying in their community and sharing their culinary talents with visitors throughout the year.

Betty Sacks is the proprietor of the Round Top Mercantile. She and husband Ronny offer a real country atmosphere, friendly and completely true to its name "mercantile." Their delicatessen serves delicious sand-wiches that many say are better than anything they can find in the big cities. Betty and her staff prepare around 500 sandwiches for our dealer lunch on set-up day. Although stretched to the limits on Antiques Fair weekends, their commitment to service to the community is unbending and everyone receives the same courteous treatment. Ronny and Betty perform so many behind-the-scenes services for us during this weekend that words almost fail me. Their energy is unlimited and their interest is in seeing that everyone who visits Round Top at any time leaves with happy memories and an experience they plan to repeat.

Publishers, Editors, Reporters and Writers...

In order to express my appreciation for the interest and support we have had from all of the newspapers and trade publications who have contributed to our success, I would have to list all of the newspapers in the state of Texas. The trade publications which have brought national attention to what started as the little Texas show in the country have my heartfelt thanks and I want to mention a few: Linda Monko, Publisher, *Antiques West*, San Francisco, California and Cape Porpoise, Maine; Chuck Muller, Editor, *Antique Review*, Worthington, Ohio; Scudder Smith, Publisher and Laura Beach, Editor, *Antiques and The Arts Weekly*, Newtown, Connecticut; Bill Alexander, Publisher, *Antiques Gazette*, Hammond, Louisiana; Jody Young, Editor, *The Antique Journal*, Ware, Massachusetts, Anne Ireland,

Southern Antiques, Monroe, Georgia; Sally and Samuel Pennington, Editor and Publisher, respectively, *Maine Antique Digest*, Waldoboro, Maine; Linda Dallas, *Antiques Gazette*, Nashville, Tennessee; Nancy Battaglia, New York, New York; Gary Ford, Travel Writer, *Southern Living* magazine; Katherine Pearson, Editor and John Villani, feature writer of *Southern Accents*, Birmingham, Alabama; *Houston Chronicle* In Fashion Editor Linda Gillan Griffin, former Society Editor Betty Ewing, Feature Editor Jane Marshall, Columnist Thom Marshall and Pamela Lewis, Design Editor of the *Houston Post*.

Other publications and their writers who have played such a major role in our growth, and who have respected the difficult role of our exhibitors who go to so much effort to be with us, are mentioned in other chapters of this book.

And a Final Few...

There is a special group of people, some local and some longtime weekenders who have shown their support for the show from the very beginning. Among them are Virginia and Robin Elverson, Lois Kolkhorst of the Washington County Chamber of Commerce, the entire staff of the LaGrange Chamber of Commerce, Richard Barton, Aileen Loehr and Louise Anzalone of the Fayette County Record, the staff of the Navasota Chamber of Commerce, Lee and Robert Cochran, June Painter, Pastor Milroy and Sugar Gregor, Barbara Dillingham Moore, Toddy and Paul Schenck, Camille and Ray Hankamer, Dick and Sherry Peck, Euphanel and Nick Goad of the beautiful Round Top Retreat, and all of the thoughtful local families who prune and trim their properties in preparation for our weekend.

Emma Lee Turney

◆◆◆◆◆◆◆

The Ghost of Round Top and

The Mad Hatter Table restaurant

Long into the night Kathleen Whatley and her daughter Christina were putting finishing touches on their little tearoom in a building which long ago had been Schulze's Brewery of Round Top. Its deep cellar with wooden floor and often-damp limestone walls is used for storage but also holds the original mash pot.

"I was hanging scrim over the fireplace," said Kathleen, "when for no reason my foot-stool flipped out from under me. It landed in the fireplace and I landed on the stone hearth. I said, 'That's it, I'm going home!'" Christina encouraged her to do just that, but because opening day for the tearoom was upon them, elected to continue working alone.

At 2 a.m., as she stood rolling up ribbon near the sofa, she froze at the sound of footsteps coming up the cellar stairs. A bearded man appeared in the doorway. He wore a collarless white shirt with the sleeves rolled up. His dark pants were tucked into old-fashioned boots. He looked as if he belonged in a vintage photograph.

The man said nothing, but Christina managed a terrified squeal. The man turned and went back down the stairs.

In describing the encounter to her mother, Christina decided she had seen a ghost. They speculated that it must have been the ghost of the old Braumeister.

Since then, his footsteps have been heard below on occasion. At least three people have reported feeling "a presence" and recently Kathleen and her kitchen helpers heard a woman's voice upstairs, and 20 minutes later, a man's voice. "We looked all around, even outside, but there was no one."

Kathleen, who has upgraded the tearoom to The Mad Hatter Table restaurant, insists that she is not given to flights of fancy but claims that there are times after hours when she doesn't feel quite welcome. "The ghost is not malevolent," she said. "He just wants to be left alone." Meanwhile, whenever anything unforeseen or goofy happens at the restaurant, Kathleen and her helpers are quick to blame Herr Braumeister.

Sketch by Charles Pfister, Courtesy, Houston Chronicle

CHAPTER TWELVE

Source Directory – Simply the Best of the Best

♦ ♦ ♦ ♦ ♦ ♦ ♦

QUITE OFTEN collectors ask antiques dealers "Where do you find these things?" One dealer was overheard to say "I'll tell you my age right on the nose, my weight within twenty or so pounds, but I won't tell you my sources!"

One of the many purposes of this book was to provide sources for you, the reader. Listed on the next pages you'll find most of the exhibitors who have shown in the Round Top Antiques Fair over the past thirty years. They still go on special buying trips to bring fresh merchandise to the show. They buy and put things aside all year long, "just for Round Top." They are simply the best of the best.

Antiques Dealers *It's always best to call ahead!*

Shirley V. Harris
Cobweb Antiques
133 Robin Road
Madison, Alabama 35758
205-837-2376
Primitives, Cabinets,
Painted Furniture, Smalls
By Appointment Only

Ann & Jim Pyburn
259 Longview Drive
Jasper, Alabama 35504
205-387-8054
American Country and
Primitive Furniture

Joanne & Bill Shipp
Paddlewheel Antiques
3920 Camellia Drive
Mobile, Alabama 36693
334-666-2801
Southern Furniture,
Pottery, Quilts
By Appointment Only

James & Susan White
Bay House Antiques
P.O. Box 9675
Mobile, Alabama 36695
334-666-7143
Staffordshire, Majolica,
Flow Blue, Mason's
Ironstone, Derby
By Appointment Only

Herbeth Collier
Collier Antiques
P.O. Box 266
Dillon Beach, California
94929
"We sell objects that move
our hearts, objects of desire."
By Appointment Only

Mary Millman
Eton Studio
P.O. Box 5734
Berkeley, California 94705
510-655-7184
Fine American Country
Furnishings
By Appointment Only

Eleanor E. Morton
Country Cousin
Fullerton, California
714-526-7529
Quality Country Antiques

Suzanne B. Smith
S. Bancroft Smith
Clovis, California
209-299-8281
Textiles, Linens,
Quilts, Unusual Smalls,
Painted Furniture
By Appointment Only

Suzan Dentry
Suzan Dentry Antiques
Golden, Colorado
303-279-8776
Decorative Accessories
and Folk Art from the
Elegant to the Eccentric
By Appointment Only

Paul & Pat Hauke
Hauke Antiques
6312 W. 92nd Place
Westminster, Colorado
80030
303-429-5859
Early Americana,
Unusual Smalls, Furniture
By Appointment Only

Nan & David Pirnack
Boulder, Colorado
303-444-8222
Folk Art, Textiles,
Decorative Arts, Funk
By Appointment Only

Sandra Lee Buckley
30 Mile Creek Road
Old Lyme, Connecticut
06371
830-434-8166
American Country Furniture

Linda & Michael Whittemore
279 Main Street
Hampton, Connecticut
06247
860-455-9385
18th Century American
Furniture in Original
Surfaces, Early Folk Art
and Decorative Arts

An excellent example of a cross
stretcher based, one drawer,
mortise and tenon table from the
Chihuahua, Mexico area. From
a South Texas ranch, former Turney
collection. Photo, Staff.

FLORIDA

Ray & Madelyn Casper
Holly Creek
Pensacola, Florida
904-435-7826
Primitive Furniture, Country
and Garden Accessories
By Appointment Only

Sue Scott
5700 Lauder Street
Fort Myers Beach, Florida
33931
941-463-0768
Linens, Art Pottery, Holiday

Woody & Nancy Straub
Antiques & Art, Inc.
8 River Drive
Panacea, Florida 32346
904-984-5139
18th & 19th Century
Country and Period
Furniture, Accessories and
American Listed Art
By Appointment Only

Brian Tebo
Canterbury House
Antiques
1776 Canterbury Street
Jacksonville, Florida 32205
904-387-1776
Unusual Decorative
Pieces, Folk Art

GEORGIA

Mary & George Hedrick
George's Antiques
P.O. Box 82695
Atlanta, Georgia 30354
770-969-2061
Early Sewing Tools, 18th
Century Iron Cooking &
Lighting Tools, Quimper
By Appointment Only

Guy & Joyce Hutchison
Hutchison House
Antiques
725 Thomaston Street
Barnesville, Georgia 30204
770-358-3866
18th & 19th Century
American Furniture,
Paintings, Accessories
By Appointment Only

Molly G. Jumper
Decatur, Georgia
404-634-0994
Fax 404-325-1159
Southern Antiques,
Pottery, Children's Antiques,
Native American Basketry
A Speciality
By Appointment Only

Texas author Elizabeth Crook autographs her book, The Raven's Bride,
published by Doubleday, Jacqueline Kennedy Onassis, Editor. A novel about
the brief marriage of Sam Houston and Elizabeth Allen before Sam Houston's tenure
as General and first Governor of Texas. Photo, Hickey/Robertson

Jeanne L. Nash
J. Nash Antiques
Atlanta, Georgia
770-938-8503
American Primitive and
Period Furniture, Smalls
By Appointment Only

Jonathan Parks and Rose Adams Holbrook, Santa Fe, New Mexico, take a rest in front of Rose's Chimayo blanket. Photo, Hickey/Robertson

ILLINOIS

Marion Atten
Antiques at
Hillwood Farms
498 N Farwell Bridge Road
Pecatonica, Illinois 61063
815-239-2421
18th & 19th Century
American Antiques in
Original Condition
Wednesday – Sunday 11 to 5

Julia Bright
Julia Bright Antiques
1349 West Wood Street
Decatur, Illinois 62522
217-429-7971
Needlework Tools &
Accessories, English China,
Stoneware, Glassware

Judith Valenti
Judith Valenti Antiques
Oregon, Illinois
815-732-3621
Fax 815-732-4179
Garden, Architectural,
Floral Paintings, Furniture,
Decorative Arts
By Appointment Only

INDIANA

Karen Anderson
Karen Anderson
Antiques
3240 Mallard Cove Lane
Fort Wayne, Indiana 46804
219-436-1535
Fax 219-436-8611
E-mail:
kaantiques@delphi.com
Decorative Antiques,
Antiques For the Dining Table
By Appointment Only

Donna Gibson
Mt. Vernon, Indiana
812-985-0172
Old Textiles, Lace, Linens,
Fabrics, Trims, Ribbon,
Victorian Accessories, Garden,
Decorative Arts

Don & Marta Orwig
1897 SR 327
Corunna, Indiana 46730
219-281-2669
Country Painted Furniture,
American Folk Art, Quilts
By Appointment Only

Susan Parrett/Rod Lich
Parrett/Lich Antiques,
Inc.
2164 Canal Lane
Georgetown, Indiana 47122
812-951-3454
Americana, Rustic Furniture,
Folk Art, and Outsider Art

IOWA

Jerry & Linda Cron
ABC Annex Antiques
7029 Andrews Terrace
Panora, Iowa 50216
515-755-2892
American Pine Country
Furniture, Appropriate
Accessories

David & Mary Knight
Crazed Collectors
340 11th Street
Marion, Iowa 52302
319-377-5390
Old Pine Primitives,
Early Paint Pieces, Folk Art,
Quilts, Yellow Ware

A Taos Pueblo Indian painted by Howard Leigh, 1927, oil on canvas with original frame. Woody Straub, Antiques and Art, Inc., Panacea, Florida. Photo, Hickey/Robertson

KANSAS

Gina Rudolph
Keeping Room
2521 Granthurst
Topeka, Kansas 66611
913-233-0256
American Country Furniture, Pottery and Baskets
By Appointment Only

KENTUCKY

Alice (Ali) Rickstrew
The Sandpiper
624 E. 4th Street
Russellville, Kentucky 42276
502-725-9778
Early Americana, Period and High Country, Fine & Folk Art
By Appointment Only

LOUISIANA

Martha B. Dunsmore
Serendipity
507 E. Main
New Roads, Louisiana 70760
504-638-4369
American Furniture & Accessories
By Appointment Only

Brenda Genius
Best Kept Secrets
Baton Rouge, Louisiana
800-259-2378
Victorian Smalls and Antique Jewelry

Barbara P. Gill
Georgian House
P.O. Box 80772
Baton Rouge, Louisiana 70808
504-926-5732
English China, Silver, Prints, Books, Decorative Arts & Garden
Shows Only

Katie B. Johnson
Katie B. Johnson Antiques
P.O. Box 274
Westlake, Louisiana 70669
318-433-3156
Rope Beds, Early Chests, Quilts, Baskets, Advertising Tins, A Wide Category of Smalls

Toni & Toby Perkins
Clementine's
9475 Meadow Lane
Oscar, Louisiana 70762
504-638-7284
Americana and Decorative Accessories
By Appointment Only

Jewel L. Salathe
Olde Towne Antique Shoppe
840 Opelousas Avenue
New Orleans, Louisiana 70114
504-364-1300
American Country and Formal Period Furniture and Accessories
By Appointment Only

Sue Spaht
Old Homestead Antiques
Baton Rouge, Louisiana
504-343-5486
Country, Patriotic and Unusual Warm, Homey Items

MAINE

Emery Goff & Bill Carhart
The Old Barn Annex Antiques
Pumpkin Patch and Searsport Antique Mall
Route 1
Searsport, Maine
207-778-6908
Maine Country Furniture and Furnishings, Toys

Ellen Katona & Bob Lutz
231 Atlantic Highway
Northport, Maine 04849
207-338-1444
Fax 207-338-5213
American Country Furniture and Accessories, Always in Original Surfaces
By Appointment Only

Betsey Leslie
Running Brook Farm
34 Jack Hall Road
New Gloucester, Maine 04260
207-926-3708
Camp, Adirondack, Country
By Appointment Only

Don & Nancy Scothorne
Sea Crest Antiques
P.O. Box 185
Deer Isle, Maine 40627
207-348-2359
Unusual Smalls from Maine,
New England
By Appointment Only

MARYLAND

Carol, George &
Robert Meekins
Country Treasures
P.O. Box 277
Preston, Maryland 21655
410-673-2603
Fax 410-673-9195
American Original Painted
Country Furniture

John & Nancy Smith
American Sampler
P.O. Box 371
Barnesville, Maryland 20838
301-972-6250
Country Americana and
Folk Art, Painted Figural
Cast Iron Doorstops, Banks,
Bookends, Door Knockers
By Appointment Only

MASSACHUSETTS

Cheryl Curran &
Pamela Courtleigh
Courtleigh & Curran
P.O. Box 94
Newburyport, Massachusetts
01950
508-465-0264
Garden, Architectural,
Paint, Fun & Folky

Donna East
Donna East Antiques
8 Brookside Street
Worcester, Massachusetts
01604
508-752-5780
New England Primitives,
Country and Smalls
of the Period
By Appointment Only

Karen Keenan Stathis
Keenan Antiques
19 Brookside Court
Amherst, Massachusetts
01002
413-256-8452
19th Century Country
Furniture, Accessories for the
Country and City Home
By Appointment Only

MICHIGAN

Ginger James
The Granite Rooster
Antiques
Brooklyn, Michigan
517-592-6307
Country Smalls, Papier
Mache, Ironstone, Stoneware

Yvonne Schlagheck
Straw Horse Antiques
1859 Smith Road
Temperance, Michigan 48182
313-847-6171
Primitives, Country
Accessories in Paint

Phyllis & Jack Wasson
The Old Store
3980 Strickland Road
Battle Creek, Michigan
49017
616-965-5208
Stoneware, Yellow Ware,
Candy Containers,
Sewing Items
By Appointment Only

MINNESOTA

Jim & Judy Cooper
Cooper's Antiques
RR 1, Box 388
Pillager, Minnesota 56473
218-829-7012
Scandinavian, Cowboy,
Indian, Sporting,
Country Primitives
By Appointment Only

Judy Stellmach
Blue Dog Antiques
Brooklyn Park, Minnesota
612-566-8413
Painted Country
Furniture, Hooked Rugs
By Appointment Only

MISSISSIPPI

Zexa R. Alman
Z's Antiques
Meridian, Mississippi
601-483-6005
Country Furniture,
Smalls, Garden Ornaments
By Appointment Only

Gail Barnette
Stardust and Memories
Antiques
102 Fairview Drive
Vicksburg, Mississippi 39180
601-634-6584
Americana, Primitives, Folk
Art, Gardening, Architecturals
By Appointment Only

John & Carolyn Heiden
The Stitching Post
162 Parks Road
Jackson, Mississippi 39212
601-372-8204
Fax 601-948-6650
Primitive American Furniture
By Appointment Only

Joan & Curtis Moore
P.O. Box 378
Canton, Mississippi 39046
601-673-2355
American Country and
Primitive Furniture
and Accessories
By Appointment Only

Distance Lends Enchantment. And from the Land of Enchantment came
Robert F. Nichols, Santa Fe, New Mexico. Robert was one of our first
out of state antiques dealers to join the show as we expanded.
He was an excellent addition with good-looking American country furniture
in original condition, quilts and a few pieces of American Indian pottery.
Photo, Robert F. Nichols Gallery

MISSOURI

Karen Murray &
Shelby Gregory
Arrow Rock Antiques
508 Main
Arrow Rock, Missouri 65320
816-837-3333
18th & 19th Century
Furniture with an Emphasis
on Paint, Sophisticated
Country and Accessories
By Appointment Only

Julie Harris
632 Romany Road
Kansas City, Missouri 64113
816-361-5034
Vintage Sports & College
Memorabilia, Luggage, Trunks

Nedra OBrien
OBriens
P.O. Box 553
Advance, Missouri 63730
573-722-5046
Linens, Lace, Coin and
Sterling, Fantastic Smalls

Joyce Cutright & J.T. Porter
Memory Designs
P.O. Box 3033
Springfield, Missouri 65804
417-887-9844
Historical Quilts, Original
Paintings, Devotional
Items, Early Photography,
Vintage Clothing
By Appointment Only

Jim Stubblefield
Jim Stubblefield's
Antiques
Mexico, Missouri
573-581-5711
General Line of Antiques and
Custom Painted Furniture

Bo Wiechens
Antiques & Art
901 N. 2nd
St. Charles, Missouri 63301
314-949-0086
Garden, Country, Art, Folk
Art, Rare & Unusual

Nancy Lunn
Nanny Goat Antiques
2004 W. Division
Grand Island, Nebraska
68803
308-384-8686
Painted Pine Primitives,
Small Country Furniture and
Architectural Pieces

Nancy Chesterton
Newfields Country
Antiques
142 Rte 87
Newfields, New Hampshire
03856
603-778-8990
Restored Victorian Trunks,
Country and Decorative Arts
By Appointment Only

Joe & Cecelia Ewing
The Ewings
65 Federal Corner Road
Tuftonboro, New
Hampshire 03816
603-569-3861
New England Antique
Furniture, Appropriate
Accessories, Textiles, Folk Art,
Authenticity Guaranteed

John Pappas
P.O. Box 96
Weat Swanzey,
New Hampshire 03469
Fine Porcelains,
Auction Services

Everlastings. Photo, Hickey/Robertson

**Richard E. Vandall &
Wayne R. Adams**
**American Decorative
Arts**
RFD#1, Box 29
Canaan, New Hampshire
603-523-4276
Fax 603-523-4888
E-mail:
amr_dec_arts@endor.com
*Stevengraphs, Shaker
Furnishings and Early
American Country,
English Bits*

NEW JERSEY

Mable Bareiszis
Little Oxbow
33 Oxmead Road
Westhampton, New Jersey
08060
609-267-4411
*Country Furniture
and Accessories
By Appointment Only*

NEW MEXICO

Rose Adams Holbrook
Faircloth/Adams
211 Old Santa Fe Trail
Santa Fe, New Mexico 87501
505-982-8700
Fax 505-982-5115
Textiles and Linens

Robert Nichols
Robert F. Nichols
419 Canyon Road
Santa Fe, New Mexico 87501
505-982-2145
*Traditional Indian Paintings,
American Country Antiques,
Contemporary Indian Pottery*

NEW YORK

June Ainsworth
**Ainsworth Art &
Antiques**
P.O. Box 928
Southampton, New York
11969
516-324-2296
*Unique Smalls, Animal
Paintings, Good &
Unusual Furniture
By Appointment Only*

Nancy S. Boyd
Bridgehampton, New York
516-537-3838
*Mexican Decorative Arts,
Early 19th Century Furniture,
Accessories
By Appointment Only*

**Robert E. Kinnaman &
Brian A. Ramaekers, Inc.**
P.O. Box 1140
Wainscott, New York 11975
516-537-0079
516-537-3838
*American Furniture, Folk Art,
Native American Material*

Mario Pollo
19 Rondout Harbor
Port Ewen, New York 12466
1-800-539-8544
*Early American Furniture,
Accessories
By Appointment Only*

Joyce Settel
Joyce Settel, Ltd.
P.O. Box 94
Quoque, New York 11959
516-653-5670
*English Chintzware, Many
Unusual Pieces & Patterns*

NORTH CAROLINA

Rose Ann Browning
Hendersonville,
North Carolina
704-693-0309
Shop Address:
Antiques Gallery
52 Broadway
Asheville, North Carolina
28801
828-254-4054
American Antiques

Sally Dale
Sally Dale Antiques
Greensboro, North Carolina
910-282-2042

Rick & Dwan Mabrey
6401 Johnsdale Road
Raleigh, North Carolina
27615
919-872-2127
Country Furniture and
Accessories
Shows Only

Bill North
North's Antiques
Asheville, North Carolina
704-277-0228
Country Antiques, Wrought
Iron, Iron Folk Art

Michael Regan
Michael Regan Antiques
1121 Virginia Street
Greensboro, North Carolina
27401
910-275-7022
American Furniture from
William and Mary to Federal
By Appointment Only

John & Peggy Wilson
Wilson's Antiques, Inc.
271 New Stock Road
Asheville, North Carolina
28804
704-645-5880
Fax 704-645-1612
Country Smalls and Painted
Furniture
By Appointment Only

OHIO

Alan Hoops &
Steve Thompson
Snow Tyme Antiques
730 Liberty Street
Findlay, Ohio 45840
419-422-5365
Ohio Country Furniture,
Textiles, Holiday, Children's
Items, Books, Fraternal
Lodge Items

Bill & Kay Puchstein
American Heritage
Antiques
P.O. Box 236
Frankfort, Ohio 45628
614-998-5300
American Painted Furniture,
Painted Smalls
By Appointment Only

Terry Radabaugh
Terry Radabaugh
Antiques
115 S. Main Street
Van Buren, Ohio 45889
419-299-3036
Furniture, Architectural Items,
Country Accessories, Smalls
By Appointment Only

Barbara Stackhouse
Victorian Fantasy
4272 Wedgewood Drive
Austintown, Ohio 44511
330-792-4391
Victorian Textiles, Fine Hand-
made Laces, Linens, Early
Trims, Dolls, Garden Pieces

OKLAHOMA

Barbara & Charles Davis
Country Gathering
Tulsa, Oklahoma
918-494-7077
Great Blue and White
and Sponge Stoneware,
Quilts, Country Furniture
Shows Only

Wilma & Charles Frailey
Frailey's Antiques
Chouteau, Oklahoma
918-476-8884
Country Specialty
Furniture and Smalls

Phil Dutcher &
Sherri Hardy
The Antiquary, Ltd.
1325 E. 15th Street
Tulsa, Oklahoma 74120
918-582-2897
Early China, Glass,
Silver, Native American,
Furniture, Textiles,
Woodenware, Pewter

Al & Maxine Hester
The Cupboard
P.O. Box 615
Choctaw, Oklahoma 73020
405-390-2251
American Primitive Furniture
and Smalls, Toys and Quilts

Fran and Herb Kramer, Pittsford, New York, fell right into the spirit of Texas fun when they joined us for Fran to write a review of the show for Maine Antique Digest. *Fran had already shed her gold cowboy boots. Photo, Hickey/Robertson*

Pat Purviance
Days Gone By Antiques
Guthrie, Oklahoma
405-282-4343
Primitives, Pine
Furniture & Country
By Appointment Only

Evelyn & Udo Schulz
Shadowmist Farm
Antiques
6600 Acorn
Oklahoma City, Oklahoma
73151
405-771-4763
Colonial Country Furniture,
Fabrics and Accessories
By Appointment Only

PENNSYLVANIA

Lynn Allmond
Allmond Antiques
P.O. Box 384
Ephrata, Pennsylvania 17522
717-738-4966
E-mail:
sallmond@redrose.net
Toys, Advertising, Comic
Character Collectibles, Disney,
Fun Stuff

David Drummond
David Drummond, Inc.
P.O. Box 421
Lititz, Pennsylvania 17543
717-627-1619
Fax 717-627-5422
E-mail: rmill@redrose.net
American Decoration Painted
Furniture, Quilts, Overstuffed
Furniture, Garden
By Appointment Only

Skip & Effie Sheppheard
Sheppheard's Antiques
Rt. 56, Box 71
Fishertown, Pennsylvania
15539
814-839-2633
Country Furniture, Rocking
Horses, Flow Blue, Country
Store, Children's Wagons

SOUTH CAROLINA

Chuck & Judy Stark
3531 W. Springfield Drive
Florence, South Carolina
29501
803-669-3363
Country Furniture, Yellow
Ware, Other Early Pottery
By Appointment Only

TENNESSEE

Betty Fuss
Country Cupboard
Nashville, Tennessee
615-228-9866
Original Paint, Yellow Ware,
Smalls, Antique Garden Items
Shows Only

Winona R. Fletcher & Dennis
B. Longmire
Oak Ridge, Tennessee
423-483-1531
Fax 423-482-7466
Country Antiques, Smalls

TEXAS

Maryann Allums &
Nancy Zogg
A to Z Collectables
3632 Hanover
Dallas, Texas 75225
214-361-2574
Antique Furniture, Animal
Paintings, Needlework,
Leather Goods, Oriental Rugs

Barbara Anderson
The Wild Goose Chase
118B Midway
Spring, Texas 77373
281-288-9501
American Country Painted
Furniture, Accessories

Cynthia Anderson
Southwestern Elegance
P.O. Box 1362
Kerrville, Texas 78029
210-367-4749
Southwest Pottery,
Baskets, Textiles

Sallie & Wesley Anderson
The Boll Weevil
P.O. Box 129
Calvert, Texas 77837
409-364-2835
Fax 409-364-3737
*American and English
Furniture of the Late 18th
& Early 19th Century,
Porcelains, Texian Campaign,
Period Jewelry*

Natalie Andreas
"Secrets"
405 Pecan
Brenham, Texas 77833
409-836-4117
*Exceptional Quilts,
Linens and Silver*

Larry N. Bahn
The Country Gentleman
Antique Center of Texas
1001 West Loop North
Houston, Texas 77055
713-802-1110 or 713-684-4638
*Country, Formal, Decorative
Arts, Paintings, Accessories,
Folk Art, The Unusual*

Jean Baker
Vintage Accents
Wilson, Texas
806-996-5375
*Treasured Vintage Pieces
for the Home
By Appointment Only*

Shirley Baker
My Favorite Things
1824 Laurel Oaks
Richmond, Texas 77469
281-342-2315
*Christening Gowns and
Linens, Victorian &
Edwardian Textiles from
England, Europe and the
United States
By Appointment Only*

Russell Barnes
P.O. Box 141994
Austin, Texas 78714
512-835-9510
Fax 512-835-1276
*Texas Pottery and Furniture,
Lightning Rods, Arrows
and Balls, Weathervanes,
Antique Lighting, Bottles*

Robert Barrett
Our Shop
111 West Main
Johnson City, Texas 78636
830-868-2179
*Garden, Furniture, Smalls,
Always Colorful & Different
By Appointment Only*

Anne & Joe Bielstein
**Town & Country
Antiques**
Antique Pavilion
2311 Westheimer
Houston, Texas 77098
713-464-1861
Fax 713-464-9463
E-mail: tcantiques@
internetMCI.com
*Small English Antiques,
Boxes, Tea Caddies, Inkwells,
Writing Slopes*

William & Julia Bishop
Broomfields Gallery
419 N Nassau Road
Round Top, Texas 78954
409-249-3703
*American Glass, Pottery,
Furniture, Rugs*

Sarah & Joe Bondurant
Sarah's Selections
4910 Gladys Avenue
Beaumont, Texas 77706
409-898-3766
*Fine Old Furnishings
Personally Selected and
Restored*

Lynne Brody
Lynne Brody Antiques
1403 Olive Street
Georgetown, Texas 78626
512-863-7231
*Textiles, Paisleys, Antique
Jewelry, Porcelains
By Appointment Only*

Terry Browder
Terry Browder Quilts
Abilene, Texas
915-676-3135
Fax 915-676-4930
*Fine American Quilts
By Appointment Only*

Karen & Charley Buckingham
Buckingham Antiques
2120 LaDonna Court
Burleson, Texas 76028
817-295-0326
Country Furniture in
Original Paint and
Appropriate Accessories
By Appointment Only

Dan & Ruby Buie
Dan's Irresistibles
1005 N. Main
Elgin, Texas 78621
512-281-2259
Fax 512-281-4331
E-mail: wildrnes1@aol.com
Cottage-style Furniture,
Graniteware, Quilts,
Textbooks, Tea Leaf,
Primitives

Ellen & Kelley Burch
Settler's Cottage
3106 Broadmead
Houston, Texas 77025
713-666-1798
Fine American Country,
Primitive Furniture
and Collectibles from
New England to Ohio

David & Susie Butler
Simple Pleasures
405 7th Street at Main
Comfort, Texas 78013
210-995-2000
American Country Painted
Furniture, Folk Art,
Quilts, Primitives

Doris Cantrell
Doris Cantrell Antiques
Taylor Street or P.O. Box 21
New Ulm, Texas 78950
409-992-3232
Specialize in Texas
Furniture, Antiques
By Appointment Only

Cheri Carter
Jabberwocky
105 North Llano
Fredericksburg, Texas 78624
830-997-7071
Fax 830-997-9599
Antique and Vintage
Quilts and Linens, Dishes,
Home Accessories

Phil Barton & Jane Carter
Jane Carter Antiques
Fort Worth, Texas
817-451-5243
Architectural Cast Iron,
Ornamental Lawn Animals,
Fountains, Windmill Weights
By Appointment Only

Patricia Chapman
Collections
8822 McCann
Austin, Texas 78757
512-343-0339
American Indian Pots,
Baskets, Jewelry,
Textiles, Religious Items,
Fine Furniture

Antoinette L. Clede
Antoinette Clede
Antiques
Old Katy Road
Multidealer Shop
9198-B Old Katy Road
Houston, Texas 77055
713-461-8124 or 713-771-2753
18th & 19th Century
American Furniture and
Appropriate Smalls

Pamela Cole-Witt
Cole-Witt Antiques &
Estate Services
P.O. Box 11804
Fort Worth, Texas 76110
817-877-3703
Unique and Diverse Selection
of Country Smalls, Furniture,
Estate Sale Services

Mary Cone
Mary Cone Antiques
Lovers Lane Antique Market
5001 W. Lovers Lane
Dallas, Texas 75209
214-351-5656
19th Century English and
French Antiques

Paul & Shirley Cox
Cox's Antique Gallery
53 Lost Meadow Trail
Austin, Texas 78738
512-261-9444
Fax 512-261-9531
American Federal Period
Antiques and Accessories
By Appointment Only

Kathy Crow
Crow & Company
Antique Pavilion
2311 Westheimer
Houston, Texas 77098
713-524-6055
Sporting Antiques for Men
plus Classical English
Decorative Accessories

Dodie Delaney
La Cage Antiques
Antique Center of Texas
1001 W. Loop North
Houston, Texas 77055
713-688-4211
Smaller Scale Furniture,
Unusual Decorative Arts

Joe Dobbs &
Randy Nicholson
Cypress Creek Antiques
In the Comfort Common
Comfort, Texas
210-995-3030
Primitive, Painted Country
Collectibles from the
Late 1800s to Early 1900s,
Texas Furniture

Jean Doty
Jean Doty Antiques
257 S. Academy
New Braunfels, Texas 78130
210-629-4431
18th & 19th Century
American Furnishings with
Proper Small Accessories
By Appointment Only

Eileen Evans
Eileen Evans Antiques
Main Street
Chappell Hill, Texas 77426
409-830-8861
18th & Early 19th Century
American Furniture and
Decorative Accessories

Jack & Gloria Evans
The D&G Country
Cottage
Leander, Texas
512-267-0070
Antique and Collectible
Furniture, Accessories

Robert D. Fairlee
Austin, Texas
512-451-4738
Country Furniture,
Porcelains, Unusual Smalls
By Appointment Only

Bradley Ferst
Good Eye Antiques
4004 Buena Vista
Dallas, Texas 75204
214-528-2861
Decorative Arts, Garden and
Stone, Eclectic Style Popular
with Designers

Peggy Field
Empty Nest
4230 Annawood Circle
Spring, Texas 77388
281-353-7362
E-mail: jbfield@pdg.net
American Country Antiques
and Accessories
By Appointment Only

Linda Fleet
3108 Lake Pine Circle
Tyler, Texas 75707
903-566-9691
Fax 903-510-2580
E-mail: ifle@tjc.tyler.cc.tx.us
Source for the book,
Byrd Pottery, Identification
Guide by Robert Fleet

Frances Goodman
Frances Goodman
Antiques
301 Honeysuckle Lane
San Antonio, Texas 78213
210-344-9966
Miniature Playhouse, Doll
House Furniture, Salesman's
Samples, Fine Toy China
By Appointment Only

Gayle Green
Glen Flora, Texas
409-677-3322
Majolica, Doorstops,
Chintz, Tins, Chocolate
Molds, Decorative Smalls

Peggy Green
Alabama Antiques
3845 Dunlavy
Houston, Texas 77006
713-526-2988
Fax 713-520-0640
Lamps, Rugs, Linens, Smalls,
Mirrors, Furniture, Fun
Things for Decorating

Jerry & Cissy Greene
Estancia con Dios Ranch
Goldthwaite, Texas
915-948-3558
Smalls, Paintings,
Interesting Mix
By Appointment Only

Mary & Harold Groner
Aunt Mary's
P.O. Box 294
Sulphur Springs, Texas 75483
903-439-0432
Country Furnishings,
Decorator Items, Architectural
& Garden Accents

Ann Gunnells
Ann Gunnells Antiques
635 Pine Circle
Seabrook, Texas 77586
281-474-4544
Exceptional Architecturals,
Country, The Unusual
By Appointment Only

Tom, Bette & Susan
Gustavson
Wild Goose Antiques
Austin, Texas
512-282-1158
American Country Furniture,
Dolls, Decorative Items

Constance Haenggi
Richards Antiques
Houston, Texas
713-667-5063
Antique and Collectible Toys,
American Furniture and
Decorative Arts
By Appointment Only

Ric Hajovsky
Pan-American Traders
P.O. Box 19362
Houston, Texas 77224
281-496-7201
Central and South American
Ethnographic Material
By Appointment Only

Charlie Ham
Cedar Run Antiques
Montalba, Texas
903-549-3337
Real Western and Cowboy,
Country Antiques
By Appointment Only

Jane Ham
Hamstead Country
Things
Rt. 1, Box 9
Montalba, Texas 75853
903-549-2547
Rare, One-of-a-Kind
American Country with
an Emphasis on Smalls
By Appointment Only

Cathy & Mike Harmon
Harmon's Antiques
Rt. 1, Box 274
Campbell, Texas 75422
903-862-3351
Architectural and
Garden Pieces
By Appointment Only

Coco Harrison
Coco's
Houston, Texas
713-464-2219
Paintings, Smalls

Jack Henson
Henson Collection
Marketplatz in Comfort,
Texas
210-684-2517
Collectors Pattern Glass,
Country Furniture and
General Americana

Radene Hensz
Uptown-Downtown
317 East Jackson
Harlingen, Texas 78550
956-423-7030
Paintings, Rugs, Transferware,
Decorative Accessories

Grace Homan
Grace Homan Antiques
3303 Glenview
Austin, Texas 78703
512-472-7366
Early Period Country and
Formal Furniture, Decorative
Arts, Proper Smalls
By Appointment Only

Patti Howell
Tinhorn Traders
1608 S. Congress Avenue
Austin, Texas 78704
512-444-3644
E-mail: patima@aol.com
Unusual Folk Art, Early Texas
and American Antiques,
Mexican and Indian Silver

Ann Hundley
Ann Hundley Antiques
28407 Morton Road
Katy, Texas 77493
281-391-8643
18th & 19th Century
American Country
Furniture, Accessories
By Appointment Only

Patti & Jack Hurt
Patty & Jack Hurt
Antiques
10035 Sugar Hill
Houston, Texas 77042
713-977-8879
Fax 713-747-7418
White Ironstone, Staffordshire,
Transferware, Early 19th
Century American Furniture
By Appointment Only

Barbara Irwin
Irwin Antiques
8105 Crabtree Cove
Austin, Texas 78750
512-502-0797
Fax 512-502-1117
E-mail: irwin@kdi.com
Painted Country Furniture,
Smalls

Deborah Johnson
Village Peddler, Inc.
20223 Laurel Lock Drive
Katy, Texas 77450
281-492-0938
Antique Pine,
Christmas Collectibles,
Toys and Accessories

Gaynor D. Johnson
Gaynor's
6230 Pebble Beach
Houston, Texas 77069
281-444-9261
Flow Blue, Linens, Lace,
Unusual One of a Kind Items

Phoebe Johnson
Interiors
4829 Switch Willo
Austin, Texas 78727
512-345-4214
Antique Furniture, Accessories,
Interior Design
By Appointment Only

Dan & Maryanne Jones
Hilltop House Antiques
Austin, Texas
512-261-0044
Sporting, Nautical and
Scientific Antiques,
Accessories, Collectibles

Rick Jones
Houston, Texas
713-520-6277
Antiques and Custom
Interior Design
By Appointment Only

Diane Joplin
The Brass Ring
6231 Briar Rose
Houston, Texas 77057
713-782-1942
Victorian Jewelry,
Silver, Linens

Joy Jowell
Texas General Store
2200A Bayport Boulevard
Seabrook, Texas 77586
281-474-2882
Fax 281-474-3529
Natural Designers of
Everlastings, Wreaths and
Potpourri

Lisa Kiefer
Star Antique
P.O. Box 2364
Wimberley, Texas 78676
512-847-9970
Vintage Lighting
By Appointment Only

Lois S. Klein
Lois S. Klein, ASID
6315 Bandera #B
Dallas, Texas 75225
214-692-0036
Fax 214-692-0037
19th Century Decorative
Furniture, Accessories
And Textiles
By Appointment Only

Nancy B. Krause
Nancy's Antiques
1700 Key Street
Brenham, Texas 77833
409-836-7520
Texas and American Country
Furniture and Accessories

Annette Krupala & Jeannette
Jahn
The Cricket's Corner
Rt. 5, Box 513
Hallettsville, Texas 77964
512-798-9224
Flow Blue, American Country
Furniture, Smalls
By Appointment Only

Jan Leach
Clifton House Antiques
Houston, Texas 713-465-7427
English Accessories,
Boxes, Inkstands, Victorian,
Georgian Silver and
Silverplate
By Appointment Only

Jim Lord & Bobby Dent
The Comfort Common
717 High Street or
P.O. Box 539
Comfort, Texas 78013
830-995-3030
Fax 830-995-3455
American Country Antiques,
Accessories,
Comfort Common Bed &
Breakfast

Agatha Machemehl
Aggie's Antiques
1102 East Hacienda
Bellville, Texas 77418
409-865-2510
Fine Country Furniture,
Mostly Pennsylvania
and Texas
By Appointment Only

Dallas, Texas' Ralph Willard holding an Indian Basket.
Photo, Barbara Tungate

Dorothy Bell MacLaren
Sign of the Bell
1110 Misty Lea
Houston, Texas 77090
281-444-2179
Country, Primitive,
Victorian, Flow Blue,
Children's Collectibles

Jane Anderson de Manterola
Jane Manterola Antiques
San Antonio, Texas
210-828-1867
Country Furniture, Accessories
Shows Only

Jan & Gene Marion
2935 Oak Forest Drive
Grapevine, Texas 76051
817-329-3822
Shop Location: The Mews
1708 Market Center Blvd.
Dallas, Texas 75207
214-748-9070
Garden, Architectural,
French and American
Country Furniture

Teddi Marks
Teddi Marks Antiques
P.O. Box 208, Hwy 6
Meridian, Texas 76665
254-435-2173
Fax 254-435-2673
Cowboy and Indians Antiques

Lynn H. McCleary
Farm House Antiques
P.O. Box 900
Manor, Texas 78653
512-272-8935
Early Original Painted
Country Furniture, Accessories
By Appointment Only

Roy & Paulette McGoldrick
McGoldrick's Straw Dog
Antiques
Dallas, Texas
972-444-9259
18th & 19th Century
American Furniture,
Architecturals, Early
Iron Work, Smalls
By Appointment Only

Bobbi Mercier
Antiques & Decorative
Arts
614 Sandy Port
Houston, Texas 77079
281-496-7644
Papier Mache, Tole, Antique
Prints, Decorative Arts

Texans really like those
New England firkins
stacked in graduated sizes.
Photo, Hickey/Robertson

Bill & Hellen Meyer
Hellen's Primitives
P.O. Box 770
Comfort, Texas 78013
830-995-3280
American Country Pieces
with Original Paint
By Appointment Only

Barbara Meyer
Barbara Meyer – Books
P.O. Box 1176
Georgetown, Texas 78627
512-863-4930
Rare and Out-of-Print Books,
Antique Prints and Ephemera
By Appointment Only

Zachary Miller
Zachary Miller Antiques
2685 Creek Side Court
Highland Village, Texas
75067
972-317-4826
Early American Country, Folk
Art, Stoneware and Bottles
By Appointment Only

W.A. & Saundra Montgomery
Country Elegance
P.O. Box 417
Fowlerton, Texas 78021
210-373-4458
Country Antiques and
Collectibles
By Appointment Only

Lola Morelock
Village Antiques
Bedford, Texas 76021
972-485-3821
Country Accessories, Smalls

Doris Morris
Sweet Annie
219 W. Main Street
Fredericksburg, Texas 78624
830-997-0852
American and Country
Antiques, Folk Arts,
Design Books

Nancy Mostert
8505 N. Broadway
San Antonio, Texas 78232
210-490-4773
Fine Antique Jewelry,
Political Memorabilia,
American Art Pottery
By Appointment Only

Dan & Lana Murray
Canterbury Antiques
6861 Lakewood Boulevard
Dallas, Texas 85214
214-824-3777
Unique Architectural,
Primitives, Salesman's
Samples, Rare Children's Items

Dwight Nelms
Nelms' Antiques
522 N. Rogers
Irving, Texas 75061
972-259-9634
Antique Accessories
By Appointment Only

Fred Nevill
2624 West Alabama
Houston, Texas 77098
713-529-8473
Very Fine 18th & 19th
Century American and
English Furniture,
Fine Art and Decorative
Accessories

Margy Newton
Newton Antiques
2424 Park #One
Houston, Texas 77019
713-520-1779
Fax 713-520-5706
Americana and Texana
Furniture, Unique
Decorative Items, Collectibles
Shows or By
Appointment Only

Merlin Niehaus
Merlin's Antiques
10780 FM 116
Gatesville, Texas 76528
254-865-8210
General Line Antiques,
Certified Appriaser,
Auction Service

Peggy Niggemyer
The Rafters
467 Highway 36 N
Bellville, Texas 77418
409-865-2972
Texas Primitives,
Unusual Antiques Shown
in a Log Cabin

Roberta Nolan
The Betty Lamp
Sugar Land, Texas
281-242-6880
Flow Blue, Dolls and Doll
House Furniture, Porcelains
Shows Only

John O'Neill
O'Neill-Leonard Antiques
Austin, Texas
512-328-1797
Early New England
Furniture, Pewter,
Tall Clocks, Paintings
By Appointment Only

Janet S. Overly
9456 Dartcrest Drive
Dallas, Texas 75238
214-349-9553
American Country and
Primitives

Nadine Patterson
821 Featherston Street
Cleburne, Texas 76031
817-558-0997
Country Decorative
Accessories

Janet H. Piester
just homey possessions
Houston, Texas
281-350-2753
Victorian Silver, China,
Ladies Smalls, Linens, Small
Furniture, Estates

Nate Pipes
Unicorn Antiques
Austin, Texas
512-261-7049
Metals and Treens, Samplers
and Prints, Books and Maps
By Appointment Only

Bob & Diane Potter
Antiques on High
7th & High
Comfort, Texas 78013
830-995-3662
American Antiques,
Furniture and Smalls

Jo Rader
The Angel Patch
5805 Contented Lane
Amarillo, Texas 79109
806-358-3360
Quilts, Yellow Ware, Salt
Glaze Crocks, Primitives
By Appointment Only

Denny Register
Register's Antiques
518 W. 13th Street
Houston, Texas 77008
713-802-0426
American & European
Furniture, Accessories

Dody Resnick
Lady Carlisle's Emporium
Antique Center of Texas
1001 W. Loop North
Houston, Texas 77055
713-773-2653
Fax 713-773-2650
English and American
Country, Fine Art, Paintings

Verle Rivers
Verle Rivers Antiques
Houston, Texas
713-468-7663
English Ceramics including
Staffordshire, Transferware,
Decorative Accessories
By Appointment Only

Velma & Bob Ross
Fairmeadow Antiques
P.O. Box 1315
New Ulm, Texas 78950
409-992-3360
Antique Toys, Country
Furniture and Accessories
By Appointment Only

Ann Royall
Heritage Attic
Houston, Texas
713-781-4477
American Country
Furniture, Accessories,
Quilts, Historical Items
By Appointment Only

Susie Rucker, ASID
Rucker & Rucker, Inc.
451 Everhart Road
Corpus Christi, Texas 78411
512-994-1231
Fax 512-994-1233
18th & 19th Century English
and French Country
Furnishings, Distinctive
Accessories

Ann Sams
Sometimes Boutique
Antiques Etc.
2101 W. Wadley
Midland, Texas 79705
915-682-4751
Fax 915-683-1813
Wonderful Early Things,
Textiles, Children's,
Beautiful Objects

Harry K. Scharold
H. Karl Scharold
Antiques
5243-B Buffalo Speedway
Houston, Texas 77005
713-661-3466
Fax 713-661-3404
18th & 19th Century
American Furniture, Clocks,
Lighting. We do restorations.

Betty Sewell
Betty Sewell
Collectibles
Dallas, Texas
214-559-4602
Fax 214-369-4299
Special Decorative, Garden
and Architectural Items
By Appointment Only

A field of Texas Bluebonnets, the State flower,
and Phlox Drummond. Photo, Cynthia Anderson

Margaret M. Shanks
**Garden Antiques &
Ornaments**
901 Pecan Street
Brenham, Texas 77833
409-830-0606
Fax 409-830-1940
E-mail: mshanks@
phoenix.net
*18th, 19th & Early 20th
Century English, French
and American Antiques
for the Garden, Greenhouse
and Conservatory
Please Call Ahead*

Sandra & Jim Sheffield
Antiques, Etc.
100 Harbor Circle
Georgetown, Texas 78628
512-863-0722
Fax 512-244-0331
*Primitives, Furniture,
Quilts, Linens*

Sharron Shipe
Orient Expressions
25002 Arrow Glen
San Antonio, Texas 78258
210-497-4644
*Oriental Antiques, Porcelain
Art, Jewelry, Textiles, Dolls,
Ceramics and Furniture
By Appointment Only*

Gale Sigloch
**Golden Chances
Antiques**
Houston, Texas
713-465-3964
*English & American
Silverplate, Sterling,
Boxes, Napkin Rings,
Tiffany Holloware
Shows &
By Appointment Only*

Marlyss Skipwith
Skipwith Antiques
Dallas, Texas
214-328-0235
*Needlework, Textiles,
19th Century English
and American Furniture
and Accessories*

Carleen Smith
Carleen's Collection
Dallas, Texas
972-661-1762
*Unusual Silver Pieces,
Scent Bottles, Chatelaines
and Fine Textiles*

Sheila Stallings
P.O. Box 201022
Austin, Texas 78720
512-258-8279
Fax 512-331-6996
*Estate Jewelry and Accessories
By Appointment Only*

Betty Stansbury
Farmhouse Antiques
Nederland, Texas
409-727-4017
*New England Country
Painted Furniture
and Accessories
By Appointment Only*

Gerold & Zanna Stepanek
Zanna's Antiques
Antique Pavilion
2311 Westheimer
Houston, Texas 77098
713-520-9755
*Linens, Textiles, Sewing
Collectibles, Molds,
Decorative Accessories*

Jo Anne Stout
Thistle Antiques
Bullard, Texas
903-825-3334
*Early English and French
Country Furniture and
Accessories
By Appointment Only*

Julie Teichholz
The Old Wicker Garden
6606 Snider Plaza
Dallas, Texas 75205
214-373-8241
E-mail: teicholz@
prodigy.com
*Antique Wicker Furniture,
Iron Beds, Hook Rugs, Quilts,
American Accessories*

Phyllis Tucker
Phyllis Tucker Antiques
2919 Ferndale Place
Houston, Texas 77098
713-524-0162
Fax 713-522-9259
*Antique and Modern Silver
and Fine Linens*

Barbara Tungate
**Barbara Tungate
Antiques**
P.O. Box 821285
Houston, Texas 77282
281-496-7827
Fax 281-493-2256
E-mail: bookshows@aol.com
*17th to 19th Century Original
Prints and Maps, Folk Art
By Appointment Only*

Billie Sue Turner
Turner Antiques
211 E. College Avenue
Longview, Texas 75602
903-758-2562
E-mail: bturner@
texramp.com
Furniture, Smalls,
Ladies and Other
Original Accessories

Teri & Alan Unger
Coach House Antiques
4300 S IH-35
Georgetown, Texas 78626
512-259-5268
Pine and Country Store
Fixtures, Accessories

Glenwood & Martha Vernon
Vernon's Shop
1600 Antique Lane
Brenham, Texas 77833
409-836-6408
Antiques, Pine Country
Furniture and
Appropriate Accessories
Call for Directions

Martha Waldie
Martha Waldie Antiques
Lovers Lane Antique Market
5001 Lovers Lane
Dallas, Texas 75214
214-351-5656
American Country,
Decorative Accessories,
American Indian Jewelry

Patti Walsh
P.O. Box 306
Bellville, Texas 77418
409-865-3601
18th & 19th Century
American Country Painted
Furniture and Accessories
By Appointment Only

Mary Ann Walters
Log Cabin Antiques
4200 Peggy Lane
Plano, Texas 75074
972-881-2818
E-mail: logcabin@flash.net
Antique Quilts, Mid-19th
Century to 1930s, Internet
Home Page with 40 Quilts:
http://www.flashnet/~logcabin
By Appointment Only

Ben Ward
Antique Pavilion
2311 Westheimer
Houston, Texas 77098
713-528-5155
Pre-Columbian Art, Santos
and Retablos, Early Oriental
Pottery and Porcelains,
Thai Bronzes, Holy Land
Artifacts

Rosemary Ward
Antique Pavilion
2311 Westheimer
Houston, Texas 77098
713-528-5155
Antique Lace and Vintage
Linens, Decorative Cushions
and Textiles For the Home

Olive Weimert
Parkwood Glass
Missouri City, Texas
281-261-1258
Fine Antique Dolls,
Steiff Animals, Old Books
By Appointment Only

Barbara White
Harvestings
254 Cave Creek Road
Fredericksburg, Texas 78624
210-997-4011
Decoratives, Smalls, Paint,
Textiles, Garden
By Appointment Only

Ralph Willard
5146 Ridgedale
Dallas, Texas 75206
214-826-2584
Folk Art, American Furniture,
Crazy Wild Things
By Appointment Only

Mary Wilmarth
Wilmarth's Antiques
2407 S. Hayden Street
Amarillo, Texas 79109
806-373-5680
18th & 19th Century
American Furniture and
Appropriate Accessories
By Appointment Only

Joan M. Wilson
716 Crestview
Chandler, Texas 75758
903-849-2229
Country Furniture and
Proper Small Things
By Appointment Only

California dealer Susan Smith sold this building model to a San Antonio, Texas, architect. Photo, Hickey/Robertson

Leigh Cheshire Wooldridge
Antiques by Cheshire Design
113 West Highway 83
McAllen, Texas 78501
210-686-3421
Fax 210-686-2063
E-mail: leighcw@aol.com
Garden and Architectural Pieces, Primitives and Furniture

June Worrell
June Worrell Antiques
502-506 Welch
Houston, Texas 77006
713-664-2643 or 713-529-2875
Authentic 18th & 19th Century Furnishings, Primarily American By Appointment Only

Sandra Worrell
Sandy Worrell Antiques
506 Welch
Houston, Texas 77006
713-529-2875
Good Early Things, Complete Furnishings By Appointment Only

UTAH

Stephen Johnson
Stephen Johnson Post-Columbian Antiques
P.O. Box 630162
Rockville, Utah 84763
801-772-3272
American Folk Art, Vintage Photography, Unconventional Objects After 1492 By Appointment Only

VERMONT

Bob & Annie Hoffman
Moose River Lake & Lodge Store
69 Railroad Street
St. Johnsbury, Vermont 05819
802-748-2423
Rustic Furnishings for the Home, Lodge, Camp and Cabin

VIRGINIA

Kathleen Vance &
Mark Amis
P.O.Box 169
Greenville, Virginia 24440
540-337-4812
American Painted Country Furniture, Hooked Rugs, Folk Art By Appointment Only

John L. Long
Merry Oak Antiques
Mineral, Virginia
804-556-4577
Country Americana with Original, Painted Surfaces, Quilts, Coverlets, Metals, Rag Rugs and Related Decorative Accessories By Appointment Only

THE FOLK ART FAIR features selected contemporary artisans in many areas of interest including: woodcarvers, tinsmiths, blacksmiths, custom and twig furniture makers, needle workers, creators of teddy bears and folk dolls, pottery, basketry, custom floor cloths, rugs, bird houses, vintage buttons and beads, traditional music, decoys, trade signs, lamps and sources for custom made accessories to enhance the country lifestyle.

Folk Art Fair artisans work in original, colonial and traditional styles and their creations should not be confused with the kit work and imports seen in everyday arts and crafts shows. Many exhibitors' work is represented in Folk Art Museum and gallery collections throughout the nation and each is an established artist with his own collector following.

ALABAMA

Marie Jeff
5600 8th Avenue South
Birmingham, Alabama 35212
205-595-0262
*Sculptural Figures Made
from Gourds, Things That
Make You Smile
By Appointment Only*

COLORADO

Barbara Bond
American Rugs
200 Washington #6
Denver, Colorado 80203
303-744-8565
*Pictorial Table Rugs Made
in 19th Century Manner*

ILLINOIS

Trudy MacLaren
14 North Washington
Avenue
Batavia, Illinois 60510
630-879-6825
Primitives and Folk Art

LOUISIANA

Jerry & Helen Bowman
Lace 'N Glass
Baton Rouge, Louisiana
504-768-7634
*Lace as Art, Pressed
Between Panes*

Nancy Eaves
Conceits
76 Dream Court
Metairie, Louisiana 70001
504-831-8049
E-mail:conceits@aol.com
*One-of-a-Kind Jewelry made
from Antique Found Objects
and Handmade Things*

Leah Ann Messer
**Beaucoup Designs/
Grants Row**
3733 Floyd Drive
Baton Rouge, Louisiana
70808
504-344-0280
Fax 504-344-7514
*Men's and Women's
Fashions and Accessories,
Silver Baby Items
By Appointment Only*

A collection of ice fishing lures from Michigan. Turney Collection. Photo, Hickey/Robertson

MASSACHUSETTS

Connie Sprong
C.J. Sprong & Co.
300 Pleasant Street
Northampton,
Massachusetts 01060
413-584-7440
*Country Antique Furniture
and Custom-made Furniture,
Architectural Features*

MISSOURI

Sue Skinner
S.J. Pottery
P.O. Box 111
Bethel, Missouri 63434
660-284-6549
Pottery

OHIO

Denise & Rick Pratt
Around the Bend
3436 CR 959
Loudonville, Ohio 44842
419-994-3809
*A Traditional and
Contemporary Blend of
Willow Furnishings for
Home and Garden*

PENNSYLVANIA

Kay L. Shaeff
Springhouse Peddler
1714 Limekiln Pike
Chalfont, Pennsylvania 18914
215-822-2222
Fax 215-822-8585
E-mail: robertesha@aol.com
*Traditional Pennsylvania
German Redware
and Contemporary
Folk Art Designs*

TENNESSEE

Shane Campbell
The Workshop
7000 S. Dent Road
Hixson, Tennessee 37343
423-847-9532
Folk Art, Americana

Joe & Jean Mason
P.O. Box 2974
Murfreesboro, Tennessee
37133
615-895-2258
*White Swans, Decoys, Rustic
Lodge and Cabin Signs
By Appointment Only*

TEXAS

La Nell Arndt
Nellie's
200 W. Alamo
Brenham, Texas 77833
409-830-1756
*Specialty Clothing Boutique
with 'Nellie's Too' Label
Designs, Original Paintings*

A.D. & Sherry Baker
Country Cupboards
13820 4th Street
Santa Fe, Texas 77517
409-925-3409
*Wood and Tin Folk Art,
Primitives, Rustic Small
Sconces, Bird Houses
By Appointment Only*

Sam & Paulette Barr
Cabin Fever
536 Bonham
Columbus, Texas 78934
409-732-8162
*Antique Furniture and
Accessories with Accents on
'Cowboy Chic' and
Rustic Lodge Styles
By Appointment Only*

Jan Borron
Keep Sake
Fredericksburg, Texas
210-990-8187
Fax 210-997-6923
*Unique Ladies
Apparel and Accessories
1770s Pennsylvania Log House
Bed & Breakfast*

**Sherri Sanderson &
Peggy Blocker**
A Little Room
5405 Broadway
San Antonio, Texas 78209
210-828-5567
*Needlepoint Pillows,
Trunks, Painted Furniture,
Lamps, Planters, Silver,
Antique Accessories*

Barbara Bronzoulis
**Barbara's Antique
Button Jewelry**
2902 Twin Knolls
Kingwood, Texas 77339
281-361-3368
*Victorian Button Jewelry,
with Historical Information
on Each Piece*

Pam Brunet
102 So. Cherry St.
Fredericksburg, Texas 78624
830-997-2757
Garden Antiques &
Contemporary Folk Art

Sandra Babin Conway &
Cie Conway
Southwest Traders
P.O. Box 1628
Wimberley, Texas 78676
512-847-5119
Fax 512-847-1309
Bronze Sculptures,
Leather Garments, Accessories
By Appointment Only

Cheryl Davis
Over the Garden Gate
1207 Miami Drive
Austin, Texas 78733
512-263-2530
Original Branch and
Limb Folk Art, Arbors,
Garden Ornaments

Lois Maureen Eagan
Turtledove
6645 Avalon Avenue
Dallas, Texas 75214
214-824-5432
Unique Lamps made from
Antiques and Collectibles
Gentled by Time
By Appointment Only

Alice Eichelmann
Tula Hats
3800 Wyldwood Road
Austin, Texas 78739
512-280-0458
Garden Hats and Aprons

Tiffany Foster
Goosefeathers
Corpus Christi, Texas
512-980-1388

Joyce & Bill Fuller
B&J Woodworks &
Santas
18700 Creekview Drive
Sanger, Texas 76266
940-458-7509
Fax 940-458-7875
E-mail: fuller@cooke.net
Handmade One-of-a-Kind
Santas, Custom Early
American Furniture

Rita Hall
Private Domain
Kerrville, Texas
210-896-5893
Fax 210-896-5757

Dottie Hanko
D. Hanko's Art
in Jewelry
3310 Woodbrook Lane
Sugar Land, Texas 77478
281-980-1023
Fax 281-265-4166
One-of-a-Kind Collector's
Jewelry, All Hand Made
By Appointment Only

Joannie Hensley
Rustic Treasures
9236 Hollow Way
Dallas, Texas 75220
214-739-6090
Country, Western, Folk Art,
Rustic Specialties

Darlene Hightower
Kin Folk/Bear Folk
3218 Canadian
Katy, Texas 77493
281-391-2351
Vintage Linens, Original
Folk Dolls, Artist Bears,
Doll Furniture
By Appointment Only

PJ Hornberger
Folk Artist
205 S. Washington
Round Top, Texas 78954
409-249-5955
Original Folk Art Carvings,
Primitive Paintings,
Garden Art

Anne Johnson
Tea Party Time
7447 Cambridge #44
Houston, Texas 77054
713-796-8393
Tea Sets for Tots

Candy Kellam
Adornments Unlimited
P.O. Box 140938
Dallas, Texas 75214
214-327-2417
Fax 214-327-6562
Sophisticated Ladies Fashions
with a Texas Flair

Suzie Kelley
Li'l Angels Doll Fashions
P.O. Box 1575
Brenham, Texas 77834
409-277-0913
Designer Doll Fashions
for Many Different Dolls

Dixie L. Kennedy
Kennedy Country
Properties
2600 Becker Drive
Brenham, Texas 77833
409-836-1002
Fax 409-836-6958
E-mail:kennedy@phoenix.com
Specializing in the Sale
of Fine Country Properties

Jeff Krause
The Round Top
Collection
10106 Hempstead Highway
Houston, Texas 77092
713-682-4777
Fax 713-682-5858
1-800-651-6181
Metal Accessories for the
Home and Garden

Lebba Kropp
The Kropp Collection
Rt. 2, Box 778
Hearne, Texas 77859
409-279-6030
Hand-sculpted Folkloric
Display Dolls, Lieblings™
By Appointment Only

Bonnie Lattig
B J Designs
4317 Sendero Drive
Austin, Texas 78735
512-892-1612
Fashions from Vintage Textiles
By Appointment Only

Rebecca Sue Lillico
Homespun Hearts
1411 W. 34th Street
Houston, Texas 77018
713-956-9081
American Folk Art, Custom
Wood Work, Log Houses,
Painted Baskets, Embellished
Jackets, Collectables

Ann Lind
Mama Flake's Family
P.O. Box 2581
Austin, Texas 78768
Shop: 1114 W. 6th Street
512-494-8386
Santas, Dolls, Angels,
Snowpeople

Greg Long
Windsor Chairmaker
Houston, Texas
713-668-1655
E-mail: www.frontera.com
Traditional Hand-made
Windsor Chairs by Bucks
County, Pennsylvania native
By Appointment Only

Jo Loomis
Mosaic China Art
6857 Greenwich Lane
Dallas, Texas 75230
972-774-9950
Creative Mosaics Made from
Antique China. Tables, Crosses

Milo Marks
Milo Marks Furniture
P.O. Box 208
Meridian, Texas 76665
254-435-2173
Fax 254-435-2673
Hand-carved Western-style
Furniture From Texas
Longhorns and Native
Woods. Custom Interiors
and Installation
By Appointment Only

Judith McClellan
Houston, Texas
713-684-4636
Iron Furniture, Garden
Accessories, Hand-made Old
Pine Furniture

Debbie McCullough
Plants Perfect
5405 Broadway
San Antonio, Texas 78209
210-822-0617
Garden Urns, Bird Houses,
Plant Stands, Cachepots,
Wind Chimes, Chimineas
(outdoor fireplaces), Garden
Furniture

Catherine Miles
Found Images
9th & Travis
Wichita Falls, Texas 76307
817-723-7961
Unique Images on
Clothing and Lamps

Leo & Agnes Miller
Millercraft
P.O. Box 147
Round Top, Texas 78954
409-249-5259
Rustic Cedar Furniture,
Chairs, Loveseats, Swings,
Custom Orders
By Appointment Only

Betty Moore
Come Fill Your Wagon
2249 Highway 71 West
La Grange, Texas 78945
409-968-8231
Pewter Wall Crosses,
J. Duban Ceramic Tiles,
Unique Frames, Angels

Harvin Moore
Frontera Furniture
Company
2110 Richmond Avenue
Houston, Texas 77098
713-527-8196
Fax 713-527-8198
E-mail: sales@frontera.com
Early Texas and Colonial Style
Furniture and Accessories

Catherine E. Moran
Poco Mo Designs
P.O. Box 31
Burton, Texas 77835
409-289-2735
Jewelry, Frames and
Other Items Made out
of Polymer Clay
By Appointment Only

Louise A. Mullins
Louise Antoinette
Designs
Tyler, Texas
903-839-3166
Designing Custom
Chandeliers, Lamps
and Finials with Emphasis
on Teapots, Teacups and
other Ceramics
By Appointment Only

Judy Norman
Lost Creek Gardens
104 Brookes Path
Aledo, Texas 76008
817-443-0401
Fax 817-443-0413
Natural Dried Flowers
in Antique Containers,
Garden Antiques
By Appointment Only

Lynane Plumlee
I Believe
Rt. 2, Box 414EE2
Giddings, Texas 78942
409-542-0534
Fax 409-542-1736
Primitive Papier
Mache Santas
By Appointment Only

Gloria Rasmussen
Many Monkeys Later
7309 Greenbriar
Houston, Texas 77030
713-664-8301
One-of-a-Kind Seasonal
and Animal Items –
Exquisitely Done!
By Appointment Only

James M. Schupick
The Rustique Collection
P.O. Box 741603
Houston, Texas 77274
713-777-1837
Fax 713-777-5228
E-mail:
rustique@worldnet.att.net
Bird Houses, Feeders,
Planters, Custom Bird
Homes by Request

Patricia Sisk
Folk Art Santas
15903 Estella Lane
Houston, Texas 77090
281-444-6337
Original Santas made from
Vintage Quilts, Furs and
Linens

Andrea Smith
Toys, Hearts & Promises
1012 E. Seminole Trail
Carrollton, Texas 75007
972-492-6666
Handmade Vintage
Silver Jewelry

Ned Spurlock
Traditional Sounds
4205 Stadium Drive,
Ste 150A
Fort Worth, Texas 76133
817-921-9990
Fax 817-921-9994
E-mail: tsmusic@flash.net
Instrumental Recordings
of Hammer Dulcimer Music
by Ned Spurlock

Mary Stanhope
Briar Patch
Briarfield Bed & Breakfast
219 FM 954
Round Top, Texas 78954
409-249-3973
Fax 409-249-3961
Rugs, Christmas Tree Skirts
and Baskets Crocheted from
Fabric Strips

**Shannon Brown &
Sue Stidham**
Buffalo Girls
Rt. 3, Box 1784
Georgetown, Texas 78626
512-863-8919
*Vintage Pillows and Old
Ranch Look Hand-painted
Shelves and Tables
By Appointment Only*

Karen "KK" Taylor
4S Designs
103 E. Virginia, Ste 108
McKinney, Texas 75069
972-562-5009
Fax 972-542-4207
*Designs by Local Artists and
Other Friends from the Road
Monday-Saturday 10 to 5*

Beverly Victory
Victory Scents, Inc.
5112 Spruce Street
Bellaire, Texas 77401
713-664-5757
Fax 713-668-2133
E-mail:
info@victoryscents.com
*Potpourri, Refresher Oils and
Sprays By Appointment Only*

Doug Walsh
Early Texas
329 E. Main Street
Fredericksburg, Texas 78624
830-997-1812
*Early Texas-Style Furniture
made from 100+ Year Old
Long Leaf Pine*

Karen Watson
Double K Klothing Co.
12622 CR 1254
Flint, Texas 75762
903-534-0225
*Texas Eclectic Women's
Apparel and Decorative Items
for the Home – American
Spirit with Texas Attitude*

Rosemary Watson
Turkey Ridge
Houston, Texas
281-587-0449
Custom Samplers

Ann Wheat
Ann Wheat Pace, Inc.
Houston, Texas
713-529-7715
Fax 713-529-5154
*Hand-made, Hand-painted
Majolica Ceramics
By Appointment Only*

Greta Zimmerman
Porcupine
Houston, Texas
713-439-0308

WYOMING

Grady Claire Porter
Spirit Works
1714 Morrie Avenue
Cheyenne, Wyoming 82001
307-634-7111
*Metal Folk Art for the
Garden – Animals, Birds,
Butterflies, Angels*

165

The Round Top Antiques Fair is held twice a year in three locations as shown on the map.

The spring show is always held the first weekend in April unless Easter falls on that weekend.

When that occurs, the show is held the following weekend.

The Oktoberfest show is always held the first weekend in October.

The show is three days only – Friday, Saturday and Sunday – with no early entry allowed.

There's always plenty of free parking.

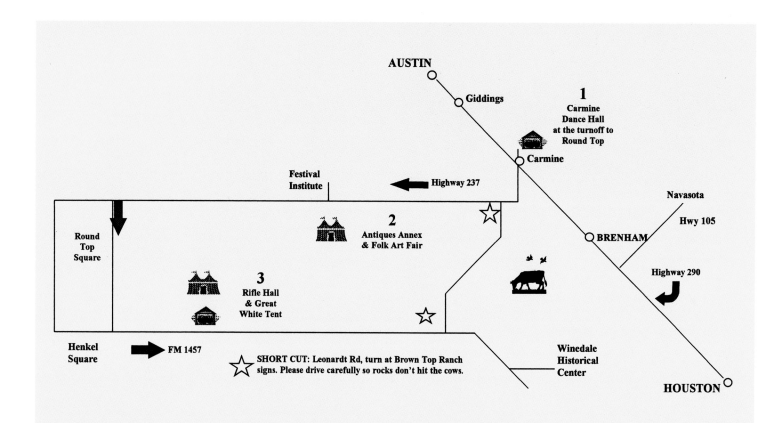

♦ ♦ ♦ ♦ ♦ ♦ ♦

The Round Top Antiques Fair
is held only at these three locations:

1 Carmine Dance Hall

2 Antiques Annex & Folk Art Fair

3 Rifle Hall & Great White Tent

♦ ♦ ♦ ♦ ♦ ♦ ♦

The Round Top Antiques Fair
is sponsored by:

Antiques Productions
P.O. Box 821289
Houston Texas 77282-1289

Emma Lee Turney
Founder and Manager

♦ ♦ ♦ ♦ ♦ ♦ ♦

So many wonderful things have happened to so many people as a result of the Round Top Antiques Fair. Many exhibitors and collectors have been featured in design articles in major national publications. The show, certainly, has received a bountiful amount of publicity over the years. And, nice things have happened for Emma Lee, too.

In 1985 and 1986, the Round Top-Carmine 4-H Club honored her for the many years of interest and support of the young people of the community. It's interesting to note that of that group of 4-H students who worked selling plants at the Antiques Fair those years, that then 4-H President Ryan Aschenbeck is now a Vice President of the Carmine State Bank. Sarah Aschenbeck is now Mrs. Kevin Bertsch and is on the staff at the Round Top State Bank. Stephanie Neumann, now Mrs. Matthew Harris, is Assistant Volleyball Coach at Abraham Baldwin Agricultural College in Tifton, Georgia. Shaun Neumann will soon be getting his degree from the Massachusetts Institute of Technology (MIT). Scott Neumann and his wife Natalie live in Red Oak, Texas, and he will receive his Masters Degree from Texas A&M University in May. Tina Wagner received her Masters Degree from Southwestern University and teaches in nearby Columbus, Texas. Emma Lee said, "We're so very proud of the young people of this community. They have not only achieved distinction in their personal lives, but many like brothers Clay and Blake Goehring often return to Round Top during the Antiques Fair to assist as parking directors or to perform other duties just to make the weekend stay successful and enjoyable for everyone."

On the twentieth anniversary of the show, Barry Moore, FAIA, of the Department of Architecture at the University of Houston, and Faith Bybee of the Texas Pioneer Arts Foundation, gave a reception in her honor at Henkel Square in Round Top. They presented her with a fine Travis Whitfield watercolor to add to her collection of Round Top scenes,

which also includes paintings by James Painter and William Anzalone.

Then, in 1992, the dealers gathered at a dinner to read a full-page advertisement they ran in Maine Antique Digest headlined "25 years of fun, food and selling, selling, selling." They presented Emma Lee with an engraved antique sterling silver bowl. For the occasion, Mayor Dave Nagel and his wife Carole issued a proclamation naming the weekend Emma Lee Turney Days and Governor Ann Richards issued a congratulatory letter on behalf of the state of Texas.

For the show's thirtieth anniversary, Emma Lee felt that book form was the best possible way to explain the phenomenon that is the Round Top Antiques Fair and to thank all of the people who have helped make this show the success it has been from the very beginning.

As she said when the final manuscript was shipped off, "If I've left anyone out, blame it on my new computer!"

◆ ◆ ◆ ◆ ◆ ◆ ◆